I0679410

Wobbled Words

Stories Inspired By Real
Life.

Compiled by
'Debayo Coker

Contributions by
Adeyemi Adeojo
'Bode Asiyanbi
Ebi Anthony
Jeff Underwood
Kate Taylor
'Lakunle Jaiyesimi
Mikail Bashir
Rasheed Adewusi
'Tobi Adebowale.

WOBBLED WORDS
Stories Inspired By Real Life.

Compiled by
'Debayo Coker
©2014

Published in Nigeria by
Beeni Publishing
381, Borno Way, Yaba,Lagos, Nigeria.
beeniglobalresources@gmail.com

ISBN: 978-978-942-917-2

Content

Acknowledgement

There are many things that are priceless; many people that are invaluable; and many relationships that are inestimable. At a very short notice, we contacted people that we believe have a passion for humanity; in turn, our contacts contacted their contacts to make this dream a reality.

We had no plan to publish any more books at this time of the year, but when Ebi Anthony handed us her manuscript, we were spurred to tell the world her passion and her need.She inspired Wobbled Words.

'Lakunle Jaiyesimi is one great guy that pulled from his pool of friendship to bring the best hands to the realization of Wobbled Words. He also made timeous submissions once he heard of this project. Thank you!

Adeyemi Adeojo ,'Bode Asiyanbi, Rasheed Adewusi and 'Tobi Adebowale are wonderful people. Despite their tight schedule, they kept to time; made artful and impactful submissions. Read them and you will marvel.

Mikail Bashir fell sick in the course of writing for this compilation yet he gave up not till he came through with his story. He told the story of peerless love and inexcusably imminent heartbreak that will come upon everyone. Read *Ode In Waiting* to see.

Jeff Underwood and Kate Taylor are two wonderful guys that I can never thank enough. Beyond writing, they shape and sharpen my dream. Kate would not appreciate my mention of this but I will apologize to her after now. She designed the skin of this book ,pro bono. While I was chatting her about a suitable title for this project, I made mention of a phrase and she picked the title, one time: Wobbled Words; and since we want stories that have real life appeal, Jeff gave the other part of the title and wrote the back matter. You two are my destiny helpers. I am always indebted to you.

My wife painstakingly took the time to proofread the draft of this compilation over and over, pointing out any error of whatsoever kind. She must have missed me those times I sat on my laptop scripting and doing all that are necessary for this publication to be a success. Thank you MyPD. I love you.

Al-Desire would look at me and raise the decibel of his vagitus to call for my attention. I would play with him briefly before giving him to his mother. Boy! I am sorry for the paucity of the affection I showed you in the course of getting this book published, I am sure you will be proud of this in good time. Love you dear son.

The cloud provided the raw materials that were employed in this publication. You are part of the cloud, just as I am.

Thank you all.

Introspection

We all tell our life experiences by unsheathing our deepest emotions through the words that we choose to let the world read or hear. Many a time, we wobble until we stumble on the right choice of words; hence, the title, WOBBLED WORDS, *STORIES INSPIRED BY REAL LIFE*.

It is either a writer ventilates the nonsense in the sense or the sense in the nonsense. Either way, there is usually something to say. Just write.

Different writers have come together to tell some of their real life experiences as stories of fact or fiction to serve as your entertainment and enlightenment, regarding different likely issues which one may face in this journey called life.

Find your favorite. There likely will be many.

The collective authors in this compilation thank you, the reader, for finding a moment in busy life to explore the creativity of a breadth of fine minds.

Our pleasure.

Enjoy.

NOT A WASTE

This journey of life
I need to find myself
Confusing compass
This journey
I lost my bearing
In the desert
In the seas
In the jungle
But what I know
I will look back
I will say
My life is not a waste
Because I will learn all that are therein to learn
I will give my best to shine the light
I will say my life isn't at all a waste.

'Debayo Coker.

iNTERLUDE

Adeyemi Adeojo

He writes under the alias HANNIBAL, was born in Lagos, Nigeria; a boisterous city that reflects the dashing picturesque in his iconoclastic stories. He holds a Bachelor degree from the prestigious OAU,Ile-Ife. He is a member of the legendary Orita Ritas. Among his numerous works, mostly unpublished, are his motley poems on *Ifepoetryportal.*

STRADDLED

The heat of the savannah form a halo hovering over the heads of scores of girls draped in dull, off colour, black and grey Jalabia and Hijab. This conspiratorial Sahel element compound the degree of forlorn these captives had been held under for the past two weeks. As beads of perspiration ooze out of the clumps of humans, the stench of sweat mixed with earth's essence and air produce one of the sickly smells ever perceived by the human nose. Yet, these captives, forcefully abducted from their dormitories in the dead of the night and led through footpaths used by the Fulani herdsmen of Chibok village, weaving a flummoxed maze through the Sambissa Forest, on the border outskirts of Nigeria with its Niger and Chad neighbours, have never for once sunk into absolute despondency as their hopes for liberation glow in pale contrast to the condition they were being held. Most of them in their teenage years and of considerable nuptial age in the Fulani custom, had gone from convention by seeking education and in turn enlightenment. Not only have they sought education, but a western one for that fact, considered a threat and thus a haram. On this hot afternoon, when humid air takes cerebral concentrate to implosive temperature in the arid land of northeast Nigeria, these scores of girls were huddled up under the intensely focused glare of the sun, with a fray looking tree whose canopy had multi eyes in readiness for the sun's romantic penetration, as the only cover avail them. The tree, like the situation of this camp, wore the dark robe of abject gloom. In this derogatory atmosphere, incoherent murmurs from the Quran's recitation which were force fed down their throats, hushed the rumblings of the heavy artillery shelling coming from the distant field, where thousands of Boko's recruits are trained and excised of human feeling. Each passing day, like the ebbing footfalls of the moon at dusk, the high hopes which the girls nurtured of regaining their freedom retrace deeper into oblivion. Days had become weeks and weeks are gradually crawling into months and hope with a little tinge of impossibility blur the vision of these girls, whose minds, though wandering, had been brought into sharp focus with the Quran verses. Cracking whips fall with callousness on the back of whoever lags in keeping up with the recitation. The uninspiring choruses subdue whatever emotion these girls have. Still, this facade reduces to sharp contrast the bland mien of the Mallam who stood in their presence with his texts containing the verses in one hand and his whip; made of tanned hide of cattle in the other. Among these girls was Safu, thirteen years of age, who had blossomed beyond her age, with Arabic beauty, unrefined as ore in its purest form and an exceptional knack for inquisitiveness. As she recites by rote the 'Alif', her eyes settle on the man before her, Sheik, the name he introduced himself by that first day of contact with them, and her mind took a dashing stroll to her world before her present predicament, only allowing her lips to perform the ritual of recitation intuitively. The sonorous sounds of the verses and its words, though not new to her, hold no meaning to her sensibility at the moment. She had been raised a moderate Muslim, with no particular emphasis on hatred or intolerance for others' views on religion. She had heard quite number of times that the commando type raids conducted by the insurgents were mainly influenced pervasively but subtly by a bias, aimed at forcefully bringing converts to the mode of extreme Islam they practice. It first started like a rumour, orphaned with no concrete validity, then it grew with no restriction, that the Jihadists conquered one town after the other, slaughtering its inhabitants and forcefully abducting its youths for propagation of its evil intention. Christians and other religions were prime target, of course, but Muslims who share none of their putrid beliefs were not spared all the same. But the beautiful town where her school was situated seem impregnable and news of Boko Haram's escapades only filtered through the gauze of the media and that alone. Not until it morphed into a monster reality right before them with the raid on her school that chilling night of April 14th. Her mind reverts to her parents, both of whom had been so bitter at the little opportunity they had at acquiring western education due to the prevalent prejudice against western education in their time, and had vowed to go the whole hog to ensure that their children never meet with the same fate. At such, they had put away every penny they earned. Her father, as a civil servant with the local authority and her mother as an ancillary nurse with the local health centre located at Damboa, a little distance from their home town of Gwoza. It had been a war between both of them when it was time for her to proceed to the Government Girls College for her secondary education, as her mother, though attuned to the prospect of acquiring education would not entertain the thought of parting with any of her children, let alone her only daughter, whose companionship she relishes. She would have preferred the Day Secondary School in their village, as this would have kept her roving eyes on her only daughter, but when her husband brought up the idea, her strong protestations met a stiffer and vehement wall of authority from her husband. In the end she had to succumb to the preponderant opinion of her husband, after several conviction by her brother-in-law, who also is an advocate of western education, especially for the girl child. Safu wondered what unspeakable agonies her parents would be going through now. She felt desolate that someone would have taken her place beside her mother in the milling shed, where they throw banters and laugh till their sides ache, when they separate the millet's grains from its chaffs in preparation of Mosa, the local delicacy. How she longs for her usual visit to Asena, her paternal grandmother, who she had been teased so many times of being a replica of both in form and gait. She enjoys the epic tales of her ancestors from her mouth, she seems to be the only custodian of the tales that bridged that chasm between the past and the present. Asena would have none of those tantrums her father throws up whenever she speaks against western education. The old woman, stuck in her ancient ways though, did little protest when she was sent away to the boarding house. She sorely missed all those fond memories of her childhood at home, and now the past weeks had nimbly eroded her innocence. She had sudden grown into the adult world of strife and wantonness, of pillage and looting; a precarious world where air as free as it abounds in nature is no longer assured the next minute. The wheezing sound of the cracking whip that descended on Busharaf, the girl few meters away from her jolted her back to life in reality and she unwillingly murmur along with other girls the texts read out to them from the Holy Quran. She has been getting used to the daily dose of abuse from these beasts, but her nerves were being stretched to a breaking point, she knew it has to be life or death as she could not adjust to this human debasement for long before she would fold up. Then abruptly, the Mallam stopped and look towards the direction of the clarion. He picked the remaining of his texts on the bare floor with the reluctance of a man over spent and heads in the direction of the camp, with his wards strutting along, all masquerading their variegated robes, journeying into yet another night of psychological torture.

The camp, sprawling makeshift Bedouin tents dotting the face of the Sambisa forest, was a quickly and shabbily assembled tentative empire in its wake. The supposed statehouse where the leader of the band of marauding Jihadists inhabits was not quite different in form or shape, but the distinction was only marked out by the Armoured Personnel Car, one of the numerous armoury looted from the Nigerian Army in their numerous guerrilla raids, parked right at the front ,and also, by the gun wielding Mujahideens who keep sentinel at this particular tent. Since, the arrival of the girls, Abubakar Sekau, has never taken the onus of seeing them. He had delegated Sheik Ibn Haruna, the Mallam, to facilitate their intensive grooming and had made all the Mujahideens aware that based on commitment, they would be entitled to have these girls whom he believed to be mostly virgins, as a reward for waging war against the Kafirs. Abubakar himself was relatively anonymous, his rise to prominence came after the death of the prime leader cum founder of the sect, Mohammed. The sect which was initially founded as a conscious pressure group, had spoken out, during most of its 'Wasii' conducted in various villages and towns in Borno, vociferously against bad governance and corrupt leaders. It was then enjoying the patronages of the power brokers, business moguls and politicians, who envisaged that it could ride on its public empathy to perpetuate themselves at the corridors of power. After the death of Mohammed, Abubakar, a reticent but radical Jihadist who was Mohammed's lieutenant took the reins and assumed the role of a more De-facto leader of the sect. He relentlessly recruits young and aspiring Jihadist, through social media by his agents, build utopian fantasies in their mind about an Islamic state carved out of the ancient cities of the north and the eventuality of making Al-Janat (paradise)and being ushered by the untainted virgins so taunted, into paradise. His aggressive recruitment ploy was laced with much guile and expertise that within months of assuming the helms he had grown his empire into the most brutal force only ranked next to the deadliest terrorist organization in the world, the ISIS. He loathes the infidels with uncanny passion and brazenly brags about many he had decapitated. Such was his neck deep commitment to the cause of realisation of the state of Islam that he sees himself beyond redemption, and hence would not entertain any thought of dialogue between his sect and that of the federal government.

This evening at the camp was quite different. It was a unique night as his sentinels milled around him to watch for the umpteenth times the relay of the video shoot where he threatened to sell off the girls on CNN. It calls for celebration, he thought. His plans of riveting the eye of the world to his cause was finally getting the international attention he craves. He is in elated mood as he walks majestically to the tent where all the girls were kept. Immediately he came in, silence, like the veil of death by the graveyard descended on the hitherto boisterous atmosphere and the girls hushed to cryptic mum.

'Howa you my yanriya? Aisalam ai-lekun. I hope you all take your lessons on the Hadith. If you do well and know that we fight for what is good in the eyes of Allah, and help us to fight, you make Al-Janat.' he said in his gruffly voice laced with unrefined intonation as he prances up and down the length of the tent.

'Book is a Haram! Do not go to school. Walahi! Yarinya, book teach you not to respect Allah. Book make you wear clothes that show your body', with a grin on his face, he mischievously lifts the veil off the face of the girl by his side.

'This', he said while running his grumpy hands down the face of the trepid girl, 'is very good for you to dress, my yarinya'."Allah like it", he continued,

"Television is no good for you. You see wicked, very wicked things of America. Internet not good for you, phone no good for you. Take your Arabic studies, fight for Boko Haram, fight for Islam", he ranted for a while and suddenly stopped.

He took an interesting look around at the girls.

"Anyone beat you?"

"No", the girls chorused as he took a cynical look around his lieutenants

"You eat your food?".

"Yes".

"Ok. You have any message for your parents. I tell them, ok?".

Then, suddenly, with abrupt speed of lightening, Safu's tender but sharp penetrating voice broke the silence.

"Alhaji, phone no good, you make use of phones. Television no good you watch it. Book no good you speak English".

She was too engrossed in her inquisition that she forgot how close the sect leader was to her. His hand landed a smacking hit across her face and her body went limp.

"Take her to the dudgeon", he yelled out at his soldiers as he dashed out of the tent in fury.

Safu went blank with an illusory dart into the Arcadian scenery of her village. She was the centre of attraction at the Emir's palace. The villagers came in their hordes with the village troubadours to celebrate her homecoming. She could see the smile of triumph on her mother's face when she stood before the villagers to address them on the great benefits of giving the girl child the opportunity to access western education. As her speech was being cheered on by the enthused villagers, who were awed by the exceptional courage displayed by such a young girl, the Emir's guard, Gidado strolled over to the podium whispered into the ears of one of the village elders standing by her and ushered her into one of the inner chambers of the Emir's palace. She was awestruck to behold three white men and a white lady who burst into her face. The lady with her impeccable English, tape recorder in one hand and a microphone in the other, spoke too fast for Safu to comprehend while others tried to get a good shot of her with their gigantic cameras. But she heard those words fall like droplets from tear-laden sky; CNN, interview, escape, as she tried to piece it together. She knew they wanted to interview her on how she was abducted, on her treatment and that of other girls in the hands of the abductors, and her escape. She had a lot to say but no sound escaped her mouth. She opened her mouth in mime but the words were hard to come by. Her head whirls in seismic spurts and she struggles to maintain her composure. In the midst of this seeming imbalance, she enjoys the fame she had brought to her little sleeping village. She was spurred back to life by the cold hug of the water that splashed a ring of pool around her, and one of the guards in his overflowing robe reeking of dirt accumulated over months of use, yelled while kicking her with the boots: "Up! Up!!", he screamed, "You infidel!".

Safu cringed as he lashed out the whip on her. Tears killed the euphoria in her and a devouring headache ate her brain with the thuds of a hammer against anvil in the hands of a blacksmith. Only then did she realize she had earlier been in a trance. She got up and for the first time had a clear glimpse of her confinement. She saw some of her mates who had earlier been taken away from the main tent. Some chattering in hush tones, others lying disinterested, while others just stared into blank space ahead expecting redemption. Then she saw her friend, Ikimat, who has never stopped crying since she was abducted. Ikimat, the only child of her parents was always top of her class. She has been disillusioned since her abduction. Safu overheard some of the men saying in Hausa dialect that she has gone mad because she refused to eat, speak to anyone or recite the Hadith during the classes under the tree. Safu has never had the chance to speak with her because the Mallam in charge had ordered her removal from the main group before she would infest the girls with her sorrows. As the guards retrace their steps from the dudgeon and shut the door behind them, emptiness descended on the girls and their days of despondency was revived. Safu, however, was determined not to get swallowed in this desperation. She saw herself as the harbinger of hope to her fellow girls, hence with pomp she stood up to address them.

"Al-salam ailekun, my sisters, I come to you all in the name of Allah, the merciful, the benevolent. Islam, our religion is never a religion of violence but of peace. If these people are truly Muslims, how come they visit so much hardship on our people?". She paused to look around. The girls countenances gave her the impetus.
She continued, "How come they slaughter the elderly and the children alike? Well, if Islam is truly a religion of liberation, how come we are in shackles, you all would ask?". Without relenting she asks further.

"How come they forcefully took us from our loved ones, exposed us to such trauma and left an indelible feeling of seething hatred in our hearts?".

"Now, I must tell you, daughters of my mother, is the time for us to seek our freedom. But we must first start with our minds. We must first liberate our minds, because the deadliest weapon in the hand of the oppressor is the mind of the oppressed. As for me, I will never allow anyone to break me down. I will stay strong till the day I gain my freedom".

As Safu finished her rallying speech she went round to lift the spirit of the girls. Some of them were too weak to be that gregarious but they managed a wry smile to reassure her she had their support.

For the first time since their abduction, that night, Ikimat spoke as Safu got to her front.

"Will I see my home again?", she asked with a deeply ingrained emotion that almost brought tears to Safu eyes.

"Yes, my friend", she responded reassuringly by wrapping her arms round her shoulders

"Insha Allah", she continues, "I have a plan, my friend. We shall. see home someday. But you must eat your food, you will need the strength for the long journey of escape".

And for a very long time, the spirits of the girls were lifted as they buzz and grin from ear to ear, recounting with nostalgia their days at Government College and how many more they would recount when they finally reunite with their families.

That night, Safu could not sleep as she overturned one plot on another in her head. She knew the onus now lies on her to bring succour to the girls. She recollects the stories of Queen Aminat of Zazzau. Her pride buoys at the thought of being Queen Aminat, riding on an immaculate horse, slashing the throats of Abubakar and his gang of looters.

She looked around at the girls, some of which had been raped multiple times since arriving at this god-forsaken forest. Tears welled up in her eyes and she feared for the worst. Silently, she recited 'Bismillahi Rahmani Raheem' and drifted into silence that conveyed her to sleep.

The next morning, Safu found out to her chagrin that the men had been coming around to take the girls away. They had carnal knowledge of these young girls brazenly. This discovery piqued Safu that she contemplated death rather than stand the forced intimacy with these filthy men and their randy urges. Then as if a scale was lifted off her eyes, she took a good look at the girls and found out two of them had slightly protruding abdomen. She stood and then went to them and asked some few questions. As she drags her heavy legs back to her sitting position, fear, the tamer of all men, gripped her and she feared the worst one more time.

Her days now become longer than her nights. She thought for a longer period than she spoke until her mind flirted with different ideas. Something kept ringing in her mind that her salvation hinges on the Mallam. She had noticed from her first few days at the makaranta under the tree with the main group, before her confinement, that he seems to have this soft spot for her. He has never hit her, even when it was obvious that she goes into blank space during Quran recitation. If only she could turn his predilection to her escape and that of her friends. She knew how impossible that would be and she smacked herself so hard with both hands on the cheeks that the girls wondered if she had seen a ghost. She stood up, pranced up and down and sat back again.

The Mallam came later in the evening, led them outside their cell to the cold embrace of freedom. This liberty though short-lived re-ignited her hope of escape. When the Mallam had taken them through the day's Hadith and asked them for questions, others were too dumbstruck with their predicament to ask. But Safu found the courage.

She raised her hand and the Mallam gesture to her to speak up.

"Sir, my friends and I would like to know the kind of man Allah is?", she said with polite innocence that got to the Mallam.

"Allah is no man, my yarinya", he responded,

"He is the supreme being that caused all to existence". He said further

"He is holy, merciful and beneficent. He is just and deals with all according to their deeds".

Looking so confused," Mallam, do you believe in Allah". She queried

"Yes , my daughter. I believe in Allah", he said," I would want you all to believe in Him and His holy prophets".

"Yes Mallam we want to believe in Allah too."

If you were Allah, Mallam, would you still keep us in this place, and beat us and rape us?". She probed on.

The unlaced words of this teenager tore into Sheik Ibn's conscience like a red hot iron smeared into the naked skins of slaves. He sniffed the stifling air around and found no solace, just the loose soil of the forest whirling under his feet. He could balk under the weight he now carries in his conscience.

Without a word, he staggered along, away from the equally befuddled girls. Suddenly, he realises in this little girl, he has finally found the courage to confront his fears. He would now decide to let his conscience speak or remain under the chains of hypocrisy which had become of his life in the last few years.

Mallam, Sheik Ibn Haruna, close lieutenant of Abubakar Shekau, the supreme ruler of the new Islamic caliphate, Boko Haram, is a very comely man in a sense. Well trimmed and clean, cerebral and vast in Islamic verses. He is the brain behind the sect's push for international recognition, expansionist ideology and negotiation for arms. His growing clout made Abubakar, who is not as refined, very uncomfortable and in no distance he saw him as a threat.

After the abduction of the girls, an expedition Mallam Ibn vehemently opposed due to his belief in the need for the sect to avoid backlash from the international community, whose sympathy he believes the sect still needs, he was put in charge of the re-orientation of the girls; a brainwashing ritual which has become their hallmark.

He saw it as a demotion, no doubt, as one of the numerous ploys to relegate him to the backdrop of irrelevance, and his disorientation with a cause he left his family for reached its apogee. Recently, he reckoned, the sect has fallen out of line, due to the high handedness of the sect's leader, his absolute power and recklessness.

Being a man of conscience, he had pointed out these things to him, and each time, he had seen it as a question of his authority and this frequent attrition pulled the men wide apart.

Things were no longer what they seem to be,.In recent times, the leadership and his recruits have taken a detour from those tenets that made him resign his lecturing post in the university, to swear an oath to defend the fledgling empire even with his life.

Now, everything is threatened. His career, his morality, his psyche, his faith and his God.

Nothing is assured anymore, not even Al-Janat that he craved so much.

He knew he had to embark on the long road to redemption where solitude is assured. Where it would be cold and lonely and his best friend would be his soul. If only he could make up for all these shortcomings with a singular act, his soul would rest.

The girls wondered why they have not had classes for almost five days now. Though, without the makaranta, life had moved on as usual. Since the arrival of Safu from the dudgeon, none of the girls had been sneaked out at night by the guards who had turned the feast of intimacy to a regular bout. Safu reasoned this had something to do with Mallam. Though having no idea of his rank among these mad men, she had observed him from afar speaking to them the last time he came, before the contact he had with them. She observed it must have been a very stern warning, as their excesses were abruptly reduced. Safu missed the Mallam. She could not understand his absence for five days.

Each passing day galvanizes her uneasiness. Her hope recedes further until she felt it totally obliterated. She was no longer her usual self, though she put up an unperturbed facade that masks an inner turmoil, however, she could still sense other girls were able to see through the charade.

Later that afternoon, Mallam came with three other guards. He looked a man so detached as he led the girls outside their confinement to their makaranta. His gaunt frame speaks a lot about what he has been going through. When he was alone with the girls, he spoke in hush voice and looked over his shoulders intermittently.

"We are not going to read much today. I quickly want

to tell you Allah does not permit anyone to suffer. Like I have always said, he is a merciful God." he spoke silently with the words spurting out in bits.

"Your lessons in life form your experience and your experience helps your survival." he continued, "I have seen what you have been going through since you arrived here. I brought three of my friends to make sure you are safe." he said

"I will be back to see you tomorrow."
The girls felt something eerie about the Mallam as he seemed too distant in thought and in speech. Just as Safu was about to inquire, he dispelled the class with a wave of hand.

As they trudge along to their strait, he pulled Safu aside and continued in the hush voice he had used all day.

"Tonight, I come to take you all from this place. It is my ultimate faith in Allah that no one is put through this indignity. It might come at a dire consequence upon my life, but I will die for my belief and you all will live." He said rather mournfully.

Safu could not fight back the tears in her eyes. She was unsure whether it was the thought of reuniting with her family or the parting with Mallam. But the Mallam sensing her heightened emotion drew her to himself and console her gently in his arms. Safu felt she would remained in the arms of the Mallam for eternity, it provided her the comfort and refuge she longed for. When the Mallam finally extricated himself, it was a jolt that terminated her childish fantasy.

"Tonight!", he enthused with finality as he races away gradually from sight

That night, all the girls could not eat their food as anxiety killed all the residual appetite they had.
Without the presence of a clock to keep time, hours seem forever. They correlate the chirping of crickets outside to the ticking arms of the clock and it heightens their anxiety further.

Later, Mallam came with a jalopy truck and six men, guns in hands with menacing looks sneaking uncomfortable glances every now and then from the slits on their turbaned heads and constantly looking over their shoulders. The Mallam entered the girls' confinement with a wide grin the girls have not seen for several weeks. He seems a fulfilled man. After ablution, he conducted the 'Ishai' prayer with the girls. Swiftly, he moved them to the truck outside, the guards jumped into the truck, and it zooms off. The driver under specific instruction evaded all the checkpoints as the rugged truck treads the chequered terrains of what used to be a game reserve; the Sambissa forest.

The Mallam sat beside the driver waving the black flag festooned with Arabic letters to beguile the insurgents who, as he is aware, will not hesitate to obliterate any on rushing vehicle without the insignia. They moved further away from the camp into the dark heart of the dreaded Sambissa forest and only met patches of checkpoints manned by lanky Jihadist frothing of alcohol and reeking of stale sweat.

They cheer and throw banters with Mallam and he in turn squeezes some notes into their hands, enough to buy them tobacco and dry gin.

It was a familiar terrain for the Mallam and his heart thuds with pride for the impact his action would have on the sect. He had absolved himself of the burden of conscience and his heart load now seems as light as a feather. This euphoria took his mind of the road for a while. His mind; a vagrant, wanders around aimlessly. He thought about Safu, a little girl of such understanding as to elicit such unrestricted emotion in him!

Lost in this euphoria, quick fire shots rang out from nowhere in the midst of the forest. Suddenly, he realized they were being ambushed. As a flurry of bullets shattered the windscreen and screams from the girls rented the air, the driver with an expertise that includes mastery of an

Armoured Personnel Car maneuvering, makes an almost about turn detour. It dawned on Mallam, they have been tailed all this while by a renegade within. This was no time to think about the culprit. He had to make a final decision. Should he retrace and give up the girls. He shuddered at such thought, as the affection he felt for Safu gulped such pettiness.

He gave a signal to the driver, who nodded in cognizance. Grabbing his pump action he jumped off the trucks with guards, eleven in all, armed to the teeth, doing the same. They opened fire in the direction of the gun men and shielded the truck as it made its way out of the Sambissa forest.

At the Boko Haram camp, words quickly spread about the capture of Mallam Sheik Ibn Haruna. He was accused of aiding the escape of infidels, of undermining the state of Islam and mutiny. Charges that carry the maximum penalty.

The next day, Shekau, led his Mujahideens, followed by the girls to witness the death of the renegade, his arch rival.

Mallam, robed in untainted loose white Jalabia, head well-shaven and shinning from the caress of the Sahel sun, looked on unperturbed, murmuring the Hadith, eyes blank and set into the horizon. As the executioner approached with his slaughter knife, Mallam let out a loud scream," I ransom my head for my haram. Allah Akbar!".

Bode Asiyanbi.

Born in Oshogbo, Western Nigeria, Bode Asiyanbi was educated at Obafemi Awololwo University, Ile-Ife and Lancaster University where he bagged a Masters degree in Creative Writing.

He is a two-time winner of the BBC African Performance Playwriting Prize and has worked with the BBC World Service as a writer on its groundbreaking radio and television drama series, *Story Story* and *Wetin Dey*.

His stage play '*Shattered*' was performed at the 2013 British Council Lagos Theatre Festival and his short story, *The Diagnosis* was a winning entry for the British Council Lagos Theatre Festival 2014. His poems are also featured in the anthology of contemporary African poetry, *A Thousand Voices Rising*.

He describes himself as a Wandering Troubadour from a long line of village weavers and palace bards; spinning colored yarns and singing out lost songs from rooftops'.

NO COUNTRY FOR FOOLS

K.T. Iraya maintains that I've always been a fool.
The world he says, is not meant for farts like me, and he
says it every time with the genuine pity of a politician.

Yet I couldn't think of anyone else to run to.

Fear. Confusion. Blankness. I couldn't hold down
why I didn't stop. Maybe I thought I could drive it out of
my mind. I only succeeded in driving it down the wrong
path. I now see everything in flashbacks as tangible as her
morning walk in the timid flickers of sunrise. I see her
fetching water in tired pails. I see her bald, bare-chested
husband, I see her bow legged little boy, I see her crossing
the potholed road and disappearing into a maze of
hurriedly plastered houses hugging each other across the
road. I see myself turning the bend. I see a petrified head. I
hear the shriek before the thud. Then the pails, water,
screeching tires and the radio stuttering Lucky Dube's *So
far so good, in this crazy world...*

"You shouldn't be sweating on this. It is nothing,
Good boy".

Good boy, that was my name back in High School
where good, gentle or religious also meant stupid.
K.T. Iraya said it was nothing. I embraced the words like a
lifeline. I held on to it until I stepped out of the ornate
embrace of his office; out of the coolness of the soundless
central air-condition system into the unforgiving din and
heated madness of the Lagos street. I saw a woman with a
pail of water on cushioned head. The words slipped out of
my grasp. I wanted to run back in but the National

Conference was about to start and he was the Chairman. He wouldn't sacrifice national time for cluelessness.

Tolu would not mind.

I avoided Eri Okan Avenue on my way to her place, electing to endure the eternal congestion on Third Mainland Bridge instead. She was not home yet so I got the key from under the wooden bench on her verandah and got in. I opened her medicine cabinet, shook out a blue vial and drugged myself to sleep.

This time the road was busy, unlike that sepia morning. BRT buses and the ubiquitous yellow danfos were roaring into the morning mist. The akara seller, with breasts like a fortress ,had set up her stand by the side of the road. I jumped the drainage and walked straight into the waiting bus. I buried my head in a book and as the bus began to move, I stole a look. Nothing. I looked again. Nothing. I breathed in relief and then it hit me as I took in air. Fetid. A parked vehicle which had now moved had blocked my earlier view. She was still there. Now twice her size. I retched like a green drunk.

K.T. Iraya maintains that I've always been a fool. This place, he says, is not meant for farts like me. I know he is wrong but I can't prove it.

Tolu removed my clothes with a diligence that could only come from a bride to be. Jacket, shirt, singlet, belt, trousers, boxers. My socks were the last because I had kicked out my shoes before the drugs choked my eyes to sleep. She led me to the tub and with those delicate hands wiped away the mess I had made of myself. I watched as she cleaned away the madness that came from my dream. From the chairs, the floor and then from herself. She didn't say a word. She tugged off the light switch and right there on the sofa we made remorseful love. I couldn't come but she did and when she did, she asked with a gasp why I had vomited out from sleep. I said nothing. She rested her head of full hair on my chest. The heaviness of guilt did not stem from sex this time. It was from the smell of death in my nose.

K.T Iraya maintains that the problem is with my head. It has always been filled with rubbish from childhood. He said my head did not fit with the world. Why would someone vomit out of a dream into life if he were normal.? K.T Iraya maintains that I am not normal. I maintain he is wrong. But I cannot prove it. I cannot.

As I drove Tolu to the office the next morning, I wondered where it had all started. I got as far as the morning and evening prayers anchored by my Catechist mother. How she knitted -in heaven, hell and the dusty fabric of morals around my forming head. I had no fontanel, my mother sewed superstitions and bible verses over it, many times with her hymnal voice choking out my ears with *The Old Rugged Cross*. K.T. Iraya said it wasn't because of mother, he said it was just because I was too soft to stand the stench of reality.

I dropped Tolu off and when I handed her the keys, she wondered why. I said I didn't want to drive anymore and I would be staying with her until after our wedding. She didn't like the idea of an emergency honeymoon. It showed in her drawn back dimples. And when she finally said it, I shrugged. I told her I would use the guest room but I was not going back to my house. She said it was not necessary. If I felt that strong about passing that same road for a reason I have refused to tell her, I could stay. I kissed her and walked all the way to my office. I love her. That is the only thing I can say now without guilt.

Mother used to say guilt is like dark rain clouds. No matter how hard I shoved the dark clouds off my mind, it always took on the form of thunderheads. And I know it would shed its burden. I know it would rain it out on my head. K.T. Iraya says I'm feeble minded. I say its meekness. He stops me as I begin to talk him through the beatitudes. He says my mind is filled with the wrong things. That is why I was never able to climb up with him.

That is why I have remained a career banker. A lifetime career of begging the rich for deposits and lying my way through crooked corners. And even this my soft head won't allow me do well.

At the office. Patrick was waiting with a problem. I had no issue with the marketing call but the route, the route was the problem. He could not understand. He has never done though. He understands nothing but deposits; every other thing he labels as excuses. He said I had no choice. It was a new account I had opened and he wanted us to do a visitation together so he could get to know the customer and of course, beg for more deposit. I kept protesting. He kept telling me he was going on leave the next day. Patrick is my manager. My manager is never wrong. He knows how to help K.T Iraya effect transfers and doctor bank statements way beyond the broken monocles of EFCC. He is no fool; he doesn't have superstitions sewn into his fontanel. He doesn't suffer panic attacks when he layers K.T Iraya's filthy lucre into phantom accounts enroute the final destination in Windhoek. My bald manager is no fool.

I swore I was going to close my eyes as we approached Eri Okan bypass, that spot where the bosomy woman with a chest like crude oil barrel sells Akara. I did but the fetor prised my eyes open. She was still there. And I saw something else; she was with a child. I blanked out. I held on to the seat as the world swirled yet everyone was passing fine, passing easy and not sparing a glance; pretending she didn't exist. They all have pretense sewn into their fontanel. They know how to survive this place. Passing people are not fools. They are not.

K.T Iraya maintains that the problem is with my head. It has always been filled with garbage from childhood. He said my head did not fit with the world. I maintain he is wrong. But I cannot prove it. I cannot.

K.T Iraya insisted he called the health services on it. I insisted nothing had changed. He said he would remind them after the conference morning session but maintained I had to grow a mind. He maintained the world is not for people like me. I disagreed. The world needs to be rid of people like him. I stopped at the thought because I was the one who needed his help at the moment. If the world didn't have him how would I get help. A simple phone call would do it but I couldn't understand why it had not. Or could it be an omen; a dark shadow creeping over my wedding. Could it be that Funke had put a hex on me for turning her face towards the twilight moon after five years of courtship. Or was it because I smirked at that popular Pastor who was accused of adultery. My mind was high on motley confusion. K.T Iraya walked into the lobby followed by his customary entourage of bloated and servile minders. He saw me, stopped and frowned.

"Brother".

He couldn't believe I came to his hotel again on same issue. He grabbed my elbow and led me to his suite. Presidential suite. Compliment of the National Conference committee. Wine. Tea. Coffee. My mouth, parched like the Atacama, needed nothing but the succor of freedom. I shook my head.

"Why are you like this Brume?"

"Like how?"

"You know what I mean. If I didn't know you well. I would say you've got bats in your belfry but I know you."

"But I did the wrong thing".

He began to laugh his politician laughter, rocking his pot belly from side to side. He said in this place there is nothing right or wrong about anything. Right or wrong is in the head and my head had always been wired the wrong way. He told me that as the chairman of the committee tasked with national dialogue he knew from the outset that the conference would fail but he announced this morning to the media that the conference would change the course of history and set the nation aright. Why? Because the allowances set aside for the conference was fifty times what he would earn as a lawmaker for the whole of his tenure. That was absolutely no doubt the right thing to do. Tangoing with the times. The simple philosophy of surviving this world of ours. And survival is right isn't it?

I didn't answer him.

I didn't say anything. I was actually tired of telling him he is wrong. The more I say it, the more he shows me the gulf between us. From the days of playing rubber balls down our dusty street, through the cracking walls of high school and the university, to where we both are presently. Violence is wrong, cheating at exams is wrong, election rigging is wrong, it is wrong to dump funds for constituency projects into your personal tax free accounts. But here he is, respected with his oratorical slyness. Here I am fleeing from my shadows.

"Go home and worry about wedding planning. You did nothing wrong"

I longed for K.T Iraya's balls.

K.T Iraya maintains that I've always been a fool. I know he is wrong but my knowing has never changed his life that looks right. Right or wrong may be in the wiring of the head. Maybe something is wrong with the wiring of the world. What about reality; about consequences. K.T Iraya says I think too hard about simple things.

He had another meeting with his party people so I went down to the lobby. I sat down. I didn't know where to go.

A text message beep told me where to go. The cabman had trouble locating the house where it was tucked behind sad palm trees in the elbow of Ikoyi. It was raining. The cab had no wipers. The cabman said someone pulled it off the previous night probably to sell it off at the spare parts market. I didn't believe him. Lying is a national pastime. He dropped me. I didn't thank him. I paid him. He said thank you.

They were in bedtime mode. Father had a leg on a low stool. Mother was adjusting the flame from the rusty lantern.

"I saw your text message". I said even before I sat down.

The Kenwood stereo was playing a raspy Fela. She looked up at me with misty eyes. She said Tolu called her. Tolu was worried about me. She began to pull out bible verses about worry from her grey head.

"Tolu said you have been acting strange. Talking in your dreams. Talking to yourself. Always afraid. She is worried. What is the problem?"

I didn't know how to say what I wanted to say until father said something about me having marriage cold feet; gearing to begin a story of how he navigated same course before he married mother. They were beaming and laughing at me when I told them. The mirth froze into wrinkled masks of shock and cautious disbelief. Mother clasped both hands to her chest. Father drew his chair to me.

"You are joking abi?"

I shook my head. "I'm not".

They didn't know what to say. I waited. They kept looking at me like a cracked urn. Then I told them what I've reasoned as the way out. Mother grabbed my hands, father began to cough. I thought his tuberculosis was back. He said no. What I just said was worse than his tuberculosis. Mother began to pull out long threads of verses from the bible, wrapping them around my tired head. She kept saying 'enemies, enemies, enemies have done this. This is how they want to ruin my wedding.' I told her it was no enemy. Father said it was her fault. She weaned me on stories of fear and hell she had dug out from the trenches of the Old Testament and the book of Revelation. He thanked God K.T Iraya had a fontanel hardened from the womb. She knelt down and began to plead. She reminded me that the bible says wisdom is profitable to direct. I should listen to godly wisdom and redirect my thoughts. I said my thoughts were directing me. I reminded her she always told me my conscience was my guide. And that was what my conscience directed. How will the husband feel, her other children, her relatives. I told them to imagine what they were going through. They were obviously too poor to take her away themselves. I reminded her one of her saying on putting others in our shoes. She stopped me midway.

"The devil himself comes as an angel of light. Do not be unaware of the devices of the enemy".

I didn't say a word again. I only nodded when father kept coughing that I should perish the thought. As I left, she had an inconsolable expression on her face, Fela was still spinning rampant words from the vinyl, mother's portable CD player was moaning 'Amazing Grace' from her room. To my ears, they both sounded the same. Maybe I'm a fool but at a point the world's expectations would always question yours. What do you do when the shapers of your expectations become the world.

K.T Iraya maintains that I've always been a fool. He says I think too hard about simple things. He says I should stop believing I'm a good person. He calls it self-deceit.

I took matters into my hand. The health officer at the council had a bad eye. The good eye had the smiles of two eyes. He was a straight man. I was straight with him.

"Why have you refused to do your job even after the Senator called your office?"

"Senator Iraya? He didn't call me. He never called my office."

I didn't believe him. K.T Iraya could lie to the nation but not to me. He smiled with his good eye. How could I be so naive. Was I a stranger in this country. How in God's name would the Senator do that. His bad eye couldn't understand my straight mouth.

I asked him what he meant.

"Sir, this local government did not vote for him. He won't pack shit for the opposition.'

I opened my mouth but closed it again. I couldn't form the words. He asked why I was so interested. I asked him why his office has refused to do the job it is paid to do. His bad eye bulged. He said their ambulance was bad and the expense form submitted would be signed when the council chairman returns from the lesser hajj. What about the deputy chairman. His good eye smiled.

'In fact he called this morning, from Jerusalem. From the Wailing Wall.'

'So you guys will do nothing till end of the month?' I didn't just get it.

He nodded. He asked again why I was so interested. He had an honest eye. But I didn't answer him. I stood up and left. We should all be at the Wailing Wall. Wailing like fools.

K.T Iraya didn't bother to deny. He said the problem is with my conscience's calibration. It is set to medieval times. He said I should go home to my fiancée and worry about simpler things. Like what I asked. My wedding he said. Simpler things are the more important things. If he were like me, he would've been too far gone. Deep-six and beyond redemption. But thank goodness he was not. He was not an abnormal fart with sanctimonious thoughts like Dead Sea scrolls. He told me how he got Annabella's company the contract to organize recruitment exercise for the National Immigration Service. It was a failure; with scores dying in stampede at the ill prepared stadium centers. There was a national uproar. The Presidency called for an inquiry. The panel sat and gave a slew of recommendations of which none was implemented. The application fee was never refunded; the dependents of the dead were not compensated; automatic employment promised their next of kin was a PR stunt. No one resigned. No one took responsibility. K.T. Iraya was the panel of inquiry chairman, Annabella was his wife. The

Immigration saga was overtaken by other national issues. People moved on. In this country people know how to move on. Even the dead. K.T Iraya told me to move on. Only fools will not learn how to move on.

I moved on my thoughts. They looked at me as if I was mad. The DPO called me aside and advised me to be wise. This could destroy my brother's reelection bid. The media would milk it for the opposition. He would allow me to retract. Though I will pay to do that. I told him I needed to pull out what I did from inside my head and this was the only way. He said why not do it in a confession box. I said I hadn't thought of it but the priest would not get her off the road and off my mind. He shook his head. I called Tolu before I handed in my phones. She cried out my call credit. The DPO was still shaking his head when I took my seat behind the station counter.

K.T Iraya maintains that I've always been a fool. Only a fool would choose conscience over survival. He would not allow my fontanel to destroy him. I call him heartless, he calls me stupid.

Father, mother, Tolu, my sisters; they all came with the same puzzlement in their sad eyes. I tried to explain I was not unhinged. They were not convinced. I am not that overly religious or morally astute but the moment I heard the sound and the body thrown up off my bonnet, a pathway opened in my head and in it the shrillness of that feral scream. The pathway closed with the scream inside my head. It only began seeping out when the cell door clanged shut.

They said I was selfish. Tolu said I was a self - centered idiot. That was the first time she got angry at me. I understood her grief. It was two days to our big day. K.T Iraya came in the evening. Tolu I was later to know had gone to weep his office down. He was the chairman of our wedding. He looked at me with the eyes of my parents. He shook his head like the DPO.

'They have removed the body Mr. Self-righteous.'

'I am grateful K.T. Thank you so...'
He told me not to thank him. He said he was doing it for himself not for me. 'Senator's brother detained for manslaughter' would be meat for the opposition newspaper. Tolu began to cry again. We had our Dubai honeymoon planned out and now I wanted to honeymoon behind iron bars. Do I even love her at all. K.T Iraya said I love only the nonsense inside my head. I thanked him again.

'I am not doing this for you.'

I started the thing about my conscience and the songs in my head, about the family of the woman, about her child, about putting her family in our shoes.

'That woman was crossing the highway in the morning. She should've used the pedestrian bridge.'

I didn't tell him I would've seen her if his party had not diverted the funds for street lighting to his election campaign. But from the way his brow furrowed, I was sure he caught my wayward thought so I kept quiet. I'm learning to unfool myself.

'That woman was a beggar. The environmental guys just told me now. An insane beggar Brume, a beggar. You want to ruin yourself because of a mad beggar.'

I looked up at him. 'A beggar?'

He left my question in the damp air. It hung there like a nauseous fart and turned to the DPO before it later fell to the cracked floor and splintered into nothingness. The DPO said if not for my brother I would've destroyed my life because of a common beggar. They don't have the time to try surefire manslaughter cases like mine when they were still busy battling Boko Haram insurgents. They allow the suspects to rot in jail. K.T Iraya left without looking at me. It's hard to change a fool he told the DPO. I had gone quiet.

He didn't know. He didn't know I was shocked too. I didn't know she was a beggar. I thought she was the woman I saw everyday with the pails in the timid flickers of sunrise. I didn't know. I felt bitter that if I had known, moving on would have been easier. I felt bitter at that truth. I felt bitter at the relief. I felt bitter at the manner I lost grasp of what I'd always *thought* I stood for. I felt bitter it took only the beggar revelation to blur the lines between me and K.T Iraya.

K.T Iraya still maintains that I've always been a fool. He said I should have known the difference. Some people are not worth the worry. Some people do not feature on conscience. There are people and there are *people*, and this country has no place for self-righteous fools who don't understand that difference. I had no reply.

THE WOMAN WITHOUT A NAME

The weaverbirds stopped their song as she received him; the boy was surprisingly light. She could even afford to shift his weight to one shoulder while using a free hand to move aside the brown threadbare curtain at the entrance of the rundown clinic. Inside, she slapped away a half dead cockroach from the bed, crushed it under her feet before smoothing the rumpled off white calico bedspread.

The rusty metal spring bed did not even creak as she laid him on it with hands long accustomed to pain, succor and the cruel stiffness of death. She pulled the doctor's chair close to the bed, wiped the dust on it with the flat of her palm, sat down and began observing him with patient eyes. Outside, the weaverbirds had begun to sing again, darting in and out of their elaborate nests in fast circles.

He had been left for dead on the desert sand. His limp form was carried to the clinic by a half-drunk palm-wine tapper who began asking at the clinic's corroded gate for the direction to the morgue. Zenatu, hearing the confusing exchange between the man and the hard-of-hearing clinic gateman from the window where she had been killing time staring at weaverbirds, hurried up to them and without a word, took the boy from the rambling man.

To her relief the boy, though unconscious, was still breathing.

As his breathing became regular, she left him to check on the other four patients inside the clinic's only ward. One had a hopeless case of meningitis; hopeless because the clinic doctor who comes once a week from

Katonga had not come in two weeks and his phone lines were dead. The man had just recently stopped seeing angels lashing out at him; all he was hearing now were dark demons calling out his name from deep pits; he had his hands perpetually over both ears and his neck was now permanently stiffened to the left. She walked past him without a word. The other three had been involved in a farming land dispute and had succeeded in physically neutralizing themselves with cudgels and machetes before anyone could come to settle their gripe. Zenatu shook her head and permitted herself a thin smile as voices of three women filtered in from the clinic kitchen behind the building. Strange, the men had nearly beheaded themselves and now, their wives were in the clinic kitchen gossiping and cooking together. Men. She went back to the boy.

The heat from the midday sun was of a vicious kind and it breathed its heated fury into the small clinic through the numerous monster cracks in the asbestos roofing. The boy began to stir, his yellow eyes flickering like the wings of a stunned housefly. She steadied him.

'Where am I?'

'Clinic.'

His lean body stiffened. 'Clinic, Injection?' The words popped out of his mouth like pebbles.

She shook her head giving him a smile of assurance.

'No injection. What is your name?'

His eyes rolled up in thought. 'Aliyu.' He finally said.

'What is the last thing you remember?'

His weak voice rose and fell as he strung the words together. Zenatu strained her ears. He had been playing police and thief with his brothers among sand dunes when someone ran into him from behind and lifted him off his feet. He didn't even remember hitting the sand.

She added four teaspoons of glucose powder to a cup of water and gave him to drink; he gulped it down with closed eyes. She watched him closely.

'I will need to take you home.' She said when he finally opened his eyes.

The boy dropped the cup on the wooden table like hot tongs and clasped both hands in plea.

'My mother will kill me… please, please let me go alone'.

'There is no point arguing my little friend.'

She left him scratching his clean shaven head and went into the theatre where the other nurse was asleep on a thin mattress spread on a rusted gurney. She tapped her awake and told her she was going to the village and would be back soon. The woman nodded without opening her eyes, and using her hands as a pillow went back to sleep.

Zenatu came out of the theatre, helped the whimpering boy to his feet, and led him out into the sweltering embrace of the bright afternoon where the weaver birds had all gone silent.

* * * * *

'Here.' He said, pointing a shaky finger. They were in front of one of the round huts scattered about a small compound. Zenatu knocked, there was no answer. She pushed at the door, it didn't't budge. She turned around only to see a lithe woman running towards them both hands on her bosom.

'Mother… ' The boy spluttered. He hid behind the nurse.

The woman stopped in front of the nurse panting. Zenatu greeted her, she responded by making to grab the boy who escaped her reach by shifting to the nurse's other leg.

'Are you the mother?'

'Yes… this boy wants to kill me before my time'.

'Madam this boy need to rest.'

'When I have not rested since morning; looking for him all over the place ehn?'

'I understand but I need to talk to you about him and it is very important.' She stressed every word.

The woman, after a moment's hesitation dropped her offensive stance and made for the door. She pried it open using a piece of wood. They entered into the semi darkness of the small hut and sat on a raffia mat in the centre of the room. The boy crouched behind the nurse. The woman was still breathing hard.

'You are the mother?' Zenatu asked again.

The woman nodded and didn't't wait for the nurse to speak before she began talking; her animated voice filling the humid enclosure. She was outside grinding millet when his brothers had scampered in too terrified to talk. When she finally squeezed the truth out of them, the terror was transferred to her by default. She ran all the way to the sand dunes where they had been playing and nearly ran mad with fear when the confused boys began circling a deep impression on the sand.

'Where is he?' She had screamed at them. The petrified boys just kept pointing trembling fingers at the impression.

'He… he was lying here.' The eldest of them stammered.

She had ran back to the village to call for help when she saw him with the nurse.

She made for him again. The nurse shielded him.

'He was nearly dead when he was brought to the clinic by a passerby.'

The woman's tattooed hands flew to her mouth.

'That's why I came with him. The force was not enough to make him unconscious...'

The woman, eyes wide with apprehension, leant towards Zenatu who was still talking. '… food. He has not been eating well and has not been drinking water too.'

The woman sat back and sighed.

'Things have been hard. I have five of them to feed and my husband is no more.' She spread out her hands in a gesture of helplessness.

Zenatu nodded. The year has been a hard one in the village. The rains have been poor. When she arrived, she couldn't't even get enough food to buy at the local market. She had to survive on the food items she brought from Katonga. The raw feeling of excitement that stirred up in her when the regional office had sent her to the village to help the dying clinic petered out with each passing day. If it was the scarcity of food alone, it would have been better. There was a strange air of intense hopelessness about the village. Everyone at the regional office thought her insane for taking the post. But the cases of VVF and infant mortality in the village had been too much for her to ignore. And from her first day at the decrepit clinic, desperate cases have thronged her. The first was that of a teenage mother of two who was knocked unconscious by her husband for dozing off during sex.

'Why didn't you tell him you were tired?' She snapped in anger.

The girl said nothing but the lines of fear on that gaunt, tearful face at the audacity of her suggestion summed up the heart of the village. It was something she couldn't't explain in words; a shadowy canopy of subjection and extant fear. Outside, a cow mooed like the slow rumble of dark clouds. Zenatu put a hand on the woman's lean shoulder.

'Beating him will make it worse. He needs a lot of rest and a lot of water with whatever he eats.' She handed her a box of multivitamin tablets from her bag and stood to her feet.

'Give him and the other children this at every meal.'

The woman took them and curtseyed in thanks. 'You are a good woman. God will reward you'.

Zenatu smiled and was already outside the hut when the woman held her by the arm and whispered.

'You are the new nurse at the clinic?'

'Yes'

The woman turned to the boy. 'Aliyu, you stay here.' The boy nodded and sat back on the mat.

She turned to the nurse. 'Please I want to show you something'.

* * * * *

They walked in silence stirring up dust with loose sandals. They walked past the deserted village school, the walled compound of the village head, past a row of burnt down huts at the outskirts of the village.

The woman stopped in front of a small isolated hut. 'You have a handkerchief?'

Zenatu brought out a brown handkerchief from her handbag and held it out to her. She shook her head and pulled down her veil to cover her nose. 'Use it to cover your nose.'

A confused Zenatu complied without a word. The woman knocked at the door and called out softly. 'It is me Amina.'

The ensuing silence was punctuated by the distant mooing of cows then the sound of moving feet. The door opened inch by inch, the hard wood squeaking against the tired mud floor. A young and frail girl peeped out. She had the harrowing look of a widowed bride.

'I brought a nurse.' Amina gestured towards Zenatu.

She allowed them in. There was only one mat in the hot interior filled with odds and ends, all which looked like her possession. They had barely settled on the mat when the odor hit the nurse; a fetid mix of stale urine and fecal smell. Both hands flew to her nose as she struggled not to vomit.

'I am sorry.' The girl said in a small voice.

Amina gave a sign. The girl sat on the bare floor and lifted up her long black robe up to her chest. One look at her, the nurse jumped off the mat and backed against the mud wall, one hand glued to her nose. The handkerchief was powerless against the relentless odor of stale urine and human excrement.

She muttered a prayer under her breath. The condition was now looking like a curse on the village. Girls with barely formed breasts, unprepared in soul and in body are thrown onto ruthless marriage mats. They struggle to birth through incipient birth canals and vaginas already scarred by the brutal knives of circumcision; a struggle that murders the tissues between the vagina and bladder or even the rectum resulting in uncontrollable leakage of urine and feces. It was the stuff of nightmares. She stood rigid like a wooden statue.

'You have to help us.' Amina held both hands out to her.

'I have seen it, I have seen it.' Zenatu breathed through the gag, motioning to her to drop her robe. She did and moved away from them to the wall which she faced with both hands to her face.

'She needs to be taken to the hospital in Katonga. That is the only place she can get help.' Zenatu said as soon as she got her breath back.

'They told us too at the clinic.' Amina paused. 'But no money to even get her there, everyone has left her.'

'How long has she been here?'

'Four years.'

Zenatu looked around the hut, then at the girl, and burst into tears.

*   *   *   *   *

She was grateful to be back outside. The cold, dusty and dry harmattan air welcomed them with intent. Amina held her robe down as the wind swept past them. Zenatu wiped her tears, the wind dried the rest.

'All those huts,' Amina whispered, sweeping her hand towards the huts scattered around, 'have someone like her in there. That's where they take them to.' Zenatu followed her hand and she felt herself trembling.

'Everyone left her to die and they are surprised she has not, even the husband.'

'She still has a husband?' Zenatu could not hide her shock.

Amina nodded.

'Where is he?'

'In the village here. He has other wives.

'He should be stoned to death.'

Amina said nothing.

'I want to see him.'

Amina turned to her, fear etched on her lean face. 'Please don't. Just help us.'

Swirling annoyance matched Zenatu's furious heartbeat. She looked the other woman straight in the eye.

'If you don't tell me where he is, I will begin asking everyone I meet on this road for the way to his house and when I find him I will tell him that you brought me there.'

Amina swallowed. She put a hand over her eyes and told her.

'Please don't tell him I told you.'

Zenatu nodded.

*   *   *   *   *

As she made her way to the compound behind the village cattle market, she got angrier; angrier because she was beginning to understand. She was beginning to see through the dark mist that was a halting presence in the village; the mask of fear on the face of her first patient, the tremor that shook the heart of the girl in the hut, the whisper-like voice of Amina, even in the way the children played in the dust. She was beginning to understand.

She entered the compound and knocked at the door of the biggest hut. She was sweating from the heat and the briskness of the walk. The raw smell of cows and decaying dung hung in the air. The door was opened by a wiry middle aged man with graying beard. He wore a long dirty tunic and had on a small skull cap. She greeted him. He contemplated her from head to toe instead of responding.

"Who do you seek?'

'One of your wives.'

'Which of them and why?'

'The one that is Amina's sister.'

'Why?'

There is something I need to give to her from Katonga.'

'She has no one there.'

'She does.'

The man regarded her again with thin eyes reddened probably by wood fire smoke or local gin
'She has gone to the farm.'

'Where is the farm? I need to see her.'

The man closed the door behind him with one hand and spoke slowly, underlining every word with a tense deliberateness that momentarily unsettled her. 'Woman, you cannot see her. The farm is far.'

Zenatu exploded. 'Why did you abandon her when you put her in that position in the first place? Why? For four years. Do you fear God at all?'

If the man was shocked, he didn't show it. He looked at her like a man in white would regard a child with palm oil on its hands. His face then gathered into a mask of annoyance.

'You come to my compound to insult me. You… a woman. Don't you have a husband at home?' Leave my house. I say leave…'

Zenatu seeing the futility of her approach, changed gear. 'But why will you abandon her for four years. She is your wife...'

'Because she brought it on herself.'

'How?' Zenatu's voice dipped in a mix of surprise and disbelief. Two little children poked out shiny heads from inside a neighboring hut. One glance from the man they disappeared.

'You are a stranger here woman, there are many things you don't understand.'

'Why don't you educate me?' Zenatu spat out, arms akimbo.

'The holy book instructs wives to be obedient to their husbands. There is punishment from God for disobeying that instruction. It is wrong for a woman to scream when she is having a child. She refused to keep quiet. Drink *tsamiya* to hasten the birth, she refused.' He continued reeling out her transgressions with a rapidity that turned Zenatu cold. She stood open mouthed and when she could take it no more; she turned her back and walked away. It was no use talking to a brick wall.

*   *   *   *   *

The sun was now directly overhead. Her veiled head throbbed as she walked.

'Fool,' she muttered under her breath 'hiding his guilt and wickedness behind old wives tales. Fool.'

A few years back, her nine year old daughter had sat on the pounding mortar in the house and she was quick to reprimand her.

'Why can't I?'
'It is a taboo.'
'Why?'

'Because it attracts evil spirits.' She replied without thought.

Her husband gave a long even stare. 'That is not true.'

It was now her turn to stare at her husband. Everyone knows sitting on a mortar is a taboo. In fact when she was young she avoided the mortar like a fiend.

Her husband was not amused.

'I beg you in the name of God do not fill my child's head with nonsense. Why didn't't you just tell her why it is a taboo to sit on the mortar?'

The truth was she had no idea. She just believed it was a taboo. And when her husband told her the reason, she felt stupid not just for accepting it but for trying to pass it on to her daughter.

The elders back then didn't want people sitting on mortars used in pounding yam; it was unhygienic. They had no better way than to weave a web of fear around it, just as they did to many other things; inventing mores which they built a nest of fear around to compel obedience; mores which with time morphed into laws, into tradition, then into belief and which almost always end up being tied to their faith and religion. It finally becomes – God said.

She turned the bend leading to the village square. A group of veiled women were crouched around a boiling pot on a wood fire.

And if the intent of the elders was to keep their women subservient, such intent would be easily wrapped in the extant toga of taboo and then passed from one generation to the next. 'It is a taboo for women to do this… God said women should not do that... '

An agama lizard bleached to near white by heat ran across her path. She stopped, allowing it to pass before continuing her walk and angry thoughts. Fear and irrational submission to men had been sneaked into the bloodline of the village with the underhand of taboo. The women were just existing, not living.

She was now getting close to Amina's compound. The raspy voice of the man was still howling in her ears. The man had dug for his wife a grave of blame with the shovel of fatuous lore. Idiot.

The door of Amina's hut opened as she got to it. She must have seen her through the crack in the door. Amina made to speak but stopped, searching for answers in Zenatu's sweaty face.

'He is insane.' Zenatu finally said. Amina said nothing. There was a brief silence. Then she spoke.

'The boy... Aliyu, she is the mother. It happened during his birth.'

Zenatu stopped.

'So he is the father?' She paused for a moment. 'Then why are you keeping her away from her son?'

'The father. Not me. But can she be a mother in her condition?'

'Is he her only child?'

Amina nodded.

'She has been robbed of her life and now you rob her of motherhood?'

'Not me nurse, not me. I take the boy like my son. She is my sister, nurse. My blood sister.' Her voice quivered.

Zenatu shook her head. She couldn't't take her mind off the image of the woman in that dark hut. She couldn't't be more than sixteen. She was a girl for God's sake. It was the worst she had seen so far. The clinic has no facility or manpower to attempt even a cursory care for her condition. She would have to find a way to get her to Katonga.

'Do you know the cause?'

'Bad childbirth'. Amina said barely audible. 'But they also say it is the curse of the gods.'

'Not any gods Amina. It is the curse of our stupidity. Do you have any female child?'

'Two. I have two.'

'Did you cut them?'

'My late husband forced me to.'

'…. and will you allow them to marry young?'

'If a suitor comes… what will I do? It is the tradition'

'Tradition… Even if the girl is twelve years?'

The woman said nothing. The nurse put a hand on her shoulder.

'Then they might both end up like your sister, so what life would you say you have lived?'

Amina bit her lips and looked down at her dusty toes. After a few seconds, she looked back up.

'Nurse… please tell me there is hope…for her….'

After a pause, Zenatu nodded, patted the woman on the shoulder and left without a word, her head filled with the image of the deathly looking girl locked away in the smelly darkness of that dank hut. She was a few meters away from the clinic when she began dialing the number of her boss to intimate him on the girl's desperate condition that was the moment she realized that she didn't even know her name.

'Debayo Coker

Born Adebayo James Oluwagbemileke Coker in Lagos, Nigeria but prefers to be called 'Debayo. He holds a Bachelor of Arts Degree in English and a Masters Degree in Public and International Affairs from Obafemi Awolowo University, Ile-Ife and University of Lagos, Akoka, Lagos, respectively. He had a foray into corporate Nigeria but his innate reflex for arts cannot be wished away as he always finds himself coming back to that point of his first love-arts.

He is the author of *Societal Fragments* and *A Man Like Me: Noteography of A Father To His Son.*

He blogs: www.pausibility.wordpress.com.

He describes himself as a wordsmith.

MY SUIT

Denver, Colorado. It is a dead wintry period of the year, when each vocalization is accompanied with a vaporized emission, in between uncontrollable gnashing, and a possible glove anesthesia; an attendant to a careless show of the wrists. It is not arrogance to decline a handshake at this time of the year. Everyone understands.

"Mr. Kibela, the hall is getting filled as guests are already waiting to meet you before your presentation." The Hotel Administrator had informed him via the intercom.

"Thank you." Kibela responded. "Can someone come up here, I need help?" ,he quickly hinted before he dropped the receiver.

Kibela had gone to Denver, Colorado for a paper presentation. He has just won one of the Africa Literary Prizes of the State of Denver. It's the first time he would be addressing an audience as august as this gathering of members of the Denver, Colorado Institute of Arts. He is there at their invitation.

"Sure, someone will be there right away" , the administrator retorted, not knowing Kibela had dropped the line on his end.

Kibela looked out of the hotel through the window. He saw that everyone was dressed in thick clothing and head warmers of different fashionable colours. He started to think he had come with the wrong set of clothing.

A knock on the door and he jolted back around.

"Good morning, Mr. Kibela. Hope you enjoyed your night?" A Caucasian lady stood right in front of him with a muffler loosely wrapped around her neck and thick hand gloves on her wrists.

"Thank you" he responded. "Are you the one to help me through my problems?" he inquired.

"Yes, I am here to serve you", she submitted.

"OK, then." He sounded a bit perturbed. "You see, I need a sponge for proper exfoliation. I don't go on a trip without carrying one, but due to the luggage size I am entitled to on this international journey, I had to shed some weight believing that I could easily get some things here. Can you help me with one?" He finished.

"But sir, you do not need full exfoliation as this time of the year. Exfoliation is done once in a while. More so, you have some moistened clothes pre-packed in the bathroom for you to clean with, if you have to wash your body at all. Most people are afraid of showers at this time of the year due to the cold weather." She educated him.

Kibela looked in bewilderment as the hostess talked him through his ridiculous need for exfoliation in this deadly cold weather condition. But who would have blamed a man of Kibela's upbringing? Your bath is not complete unless you have done a hard scrubbing of your armpits and pubic area with a hard sponge and soap. "*You do not smell clean if you don't do this each day and night*". He recollected his mama's words.

"In short, you are telling me that people go on for days without taking a proper bath, as long as the weather is like this?" he asked the friendly hostess.

"I have not for weeks, sir. I only use wipes to clean the sensitive parts." She saved him some time.

Politely, he opened the door behind her and smiled as he said, "Thank you".

"Is that all I can help you with?" the hostess probed as would be expected of any good Customer Service Representative.

"Yes, that is all." Kibela answered still leaving the door ajar.

Shutting the door behind him, he moved briskly and threw himself on the bed at the exit of the hostess. The thought of being in the same room with quite a number of people, who may not have had their bath for days, possibly weeks, even months, beat him to it. But more were his woes as he had to join the league somehow, since he would not be able to get his routine hard scrubbing done. "These people don't know that I come from an equinoctial point. The sun is my second skin." He rolled on the bed. Minutes later, a knock came on the door.

"Who is there?" he asked.

"Room service!" , the voice on the other side retorted.

Hurriedly, he jumped off the bed and wrapped himself up with his house robe as he rushed to get the door.

"Good morning, sir." A slim young Afro-politan man of average height pushed the trolley before him into the room.

"Excuse me, may I ask for a favor?" Kibela saw a solution centre in the cleaner.

"Yes, anything." the cleaner offered.

"I need a sponge for my body" , he hinted.

The young man, amidst mild laughter, looked into his trolley, and brought out a hard sponge-like material.

"Though this is not for body scrubbing but I bet it will work for what you are asking." The cleaner winked.

"We do have the sun as the second skin." All thumbs were up.

"Thank you, my brother." Kibela returned with an orgasmic expression written all over him. "You made my day." He almost hugged the young man. But he wasn't sure about the custom there and so he let it go.

The young cleaner made him know that at this time of the year, luxuriating in the bathroom is not desired by everyone, especially if there is no thermostat. In that case a mobile heater helps immensely.

Truly, a man that has not experienced the other side may not understand the other side.

Hurriedly, he had his bath the way he wanted, got dressed and ventured the banquet hall, the venue for the presentation.

He is faced with people of diverse qualifications and achievements: one could tell from the ambience of the hall.

"Good evening, Ladies and Gentlemen," he started. He had dipped his left hand into the inner pocket of his bespoke jacket; spread the sheet on the rostrum. He paused for few seconds and then continued.

"Don't mind my suit. The first time I wore it, it earned me a rent increment from my landlord." The audience chuckled.

He looked up in confusion but continued all the same.

"That is the truth. My landlord, through his Solicitor, wrote me, detailing how evasive I had been with my income. They wondered how an unknown writer earned enough to afford such a blazer." He chuckled along with the audience who are obviously more relaxed now.

He started on a note no one would have thought because he did not conform himself to the usual protocol of such an elevated audience. They must be thinking it is a new approach.

"Part of the Quit Notice reads: …AS HALF YEARLY TENANT. But I wonder if my landlord explained to his Solicitor that he never accepted half year rent from me at any time since my three year occupation of the self-contained apartment; I pay annually, latest on the 15th of January of the year in view. Even without any special legal knowledge, I know their legalese tripod is standing on one leg. My tenancy expires every 31st of December."

The audience listened on.

"I can't be thrown out of my apartment within the

year when my rent lasts till the end of the year. My tenancy subsists. Simple logic!" His index finger on his cranium.

He looked on the dais, still pretending he has a script. He did it perfectly. The audience looked on ecstatically.

"I did not broach the notice with my co-tenants. The due date of my supposed vacation of the apartment passed, and I was expecting some form of thuggery to be employed by the Solicitor and my Landlord as is usual in this context." He looked up and into the faces of the many people in the gallery. He could see distaste for the duo.

"All thanks to this suit." He adjusted the lapel smartly and smiled as he went back to reading from his script; the script he never had.

"I entertained a court bailiff for the first time in my life. He had come to serve me a Writ of Summons." His face writhed.

His two arms are on the soapbox to signify being inside the dock.

"I appeared before the Municipal Magistrate on the allotted date." His arms behind him, the gathering still enrapt in the tale. At this time, he had gained more confidence that he has them in his palms.

"The Magistrate asked," he changed his voice as he expressed huskily," Young man, why did you defy the Summons to appear before this Honorable Court on two previous occasions?" He smiled as he looked up to register his affinity with the audience.

"Me lord, I did not get any Hearing Notice from this Honorable Court."

Changes his voice to sound husky.

"Barrister Tutulipa! Is that true?" He pretended he was bespectacled to mimic the Magistrate and turned his head to look at the right direction as if addressing someone there.

He stood to one side as Barrister Tutulipa "I did serve the Summons through one of the co-tenants, though I am not sure if it were delivered to Mr. Kibela."

He got back to standing in the dock.

"Your lordship, nobody delivered any Summons to me."

He looked at the audience and spoke to them, "I wouldn't want to bore you with the story of the herd conspiracy going on in my compound. They wonder if a writer should be living amongst men."

Now his voice went back to husky. "Anyway, that is not why we are here."

"Why are you troubling the entire compound with your stereo and have endangered others by keeping dangerous pets in the house?"

"Me lord, I do not own a stereo. The Bailiff can attest to that as he entered into my apartment on the day he served me the Court Summons." he stated flatly.

"Is that so, Mr. Katunga?" He said huskily, mimicking the Magistrate.

'Yes sir!" He stepped aside, arms straight down like a soldier that had just sighted his superior and is ready to salute. "And neither did I see any pet whatsoever near his apartment." He is now at ease.

"Now it is clear to this Honorable Court that Mr. Kibela owns no stereo and keep s no pet. Prosecution, what other allegation do you have against the defendant?" He stated that in the Magistrate's voice.

The audience looked on, enthralled.

"I quickly stated that I pay my rent when due and I presented my receipts so far." He displayed some imaginary papers then.

"Mr. Kibela, I can see that you are a dutiful tenant observing your own side of the Tenancy Agreement. Good of you!" He reeled the Magistrate's conclusion, his acquittal as well as the acquiescence of the Solicitor and the Landlord.

"I went home in peace." He raised both hands.

His narration was punctuated with mild clapping from the assemblage.

He continued and the applause stopped abruptly.

"A few days later, my landlord fired his Solicitor for paucity of knowledge. Even when the Solicitor wanted him to know that their usual practice was circumvented by the new Magistrate, his plea yielded no fruit."

"Fired!" He quoted the landlord.

"That was all he got as recompense for his failure to be toady early enough to the new Magistrate." He stated with a show of pity for the Solicitor.

"After all, most of them have price tags." He quoted the old landlord.

"When I remained unmoved by the Quit Notice, he employed another strategy. The landlord brought untethered hounds to the compound, believing that since animals are easy carriers of EVD, I will run for dear life. But observing the Landlord for a few days, I found he was still strong and active, so the possibility of the hounds being carriers of the Ebola Virus was reduced. Then, I fed them, and we became pals." He displayed the frustration of the landlord and the audience released riotous sounds of laughter.

He wondered if he was being made jest of, or if he was still impacting the gathering. But not to betray his sense of misery, as he had left the actual paper he prepared for the presentation in the hotel room, he continued.

"The weekend that I befriended the dogs, my dear landlord summoned a meeting of all the tenants." He sat in the air to indicate the sitting arrangement for the meeting.

"I had told myself that no matter what happens, I will remain undaunted by whatever elements the old man may have to present. I kept my mouth shut!" He held his lips tightly. "While I just observed, especially when I knew that tale bearers abound all around me." He turned, round and about, to emphasize his submissions. "I don't want to be taken as anti." His arms went akimbo.

He shook his head, "But I could not stand the unplumbed hypocrisy. I couldn't.

"You all know I am a man of peace with principled integrity and honesty." He quoted the landlord.

"Yes sir!" the other tenants chorused sheepishly.

"I have seen that there is an ongoing division in this compound and as the head of this household I want us all to live in harmony." The landlord continued. "Henceforth, there will be an avenue for us to complain, rather than resorting to some unconventional ways of solving our issues." The landlord submitted.

He looked into the gallery, moved to the front of the rostrum.

"All the while my ears were plugged with my earphone as I was listening to songs of one of my favorite Bulawayo groups." He grimaced, "I don't want to be infected with lies or join the gallery of fawns. Hence I blocked them out, out of courtesy; courtesy to myself mainly.

"BOY!" He then expressed the noise and displayed the sudden kick from the landlord that jerked him back to life, as he was carried away chorusing the song from his mobile phone cum radio.

He adjusted his jacket, smiled and continued.

"Offhandedly, I told the old man," he cleared his throat, "Sir! My name is Kibela and any derogatory reference may not be welcomed, sir." He looked straight.

"And how am I to come into this conversation, sir?" "One of the tenants said, 'You mean you have not been listening to what we have been discussing so far?'" He multi-casted the whole scenario, just as a Robin Williams would voice-over many characters with his amazing voice in any cartoon production, better still, like a Tyler Perry and Madea ..

"The only thing I heard was, 'I am a man of peace…integrity.'"

He mimicked the jaw-dropped faces of the co-tenants, just as the audience too was jaw-dropped, listening to his account.

"I wonder when you, this lazy man that hides under penning, became rich enough to afford such an elegant three piece suit. You must be doing something funny that we all don't know about." H e quoted his landlord and detailed the agreement of the tenants that followed the statement, "They all yelled, 'YES!'"

He looked at his suit as he relished the bespokenness of it. The audience chortled.

He whispered with his right palm covering a side of his mouth as if sharing a secret, "All because of this suit for which they are not sure if I bought it on credit!" He gave a lively smile as he looked into the gallery, who are now reeling with laughter.

He drank from the glass of water that was seated on a glass stool by the side of the rostrum.

"I am still a writer as this is the path that I have chosen and this is the way that I want to go. My royalty may not have been able to buy the suit that troubles my Landlord, but the goodwill of writing and dignity of labor has brought it to me on a platter of gold." The audience stood up with great éclat. He paused to enjoy the celebration.

"One thing I want you to be sure of is that your rent will be constant as long as I occupy that apartment. The suit will not take that away from you. I told the landlord." He touched the suit again.

"May I ask you a question please?" He threw that to the audience.

"How do I look?" He asked.

The outstanding response, "GREAT!"

Astonished at the acceptance of his treatment of the audience, he concluded that he had performed greatly; joy on his face.

"Sir, you seem to have forgotten that the law is against forgery and impersonation. Also, our culture is never on the side of deceivers and liars." At the sound of his voice, there is quietude in the audience as he attempted to round off.

He moved a bit to the left side of the stage, rested his right hand on the rostrum with his arm bracing his chin.

"I spoke to my landlord in an unadulterated tranquil tone." He cleared his voice. "For the few minutes that I spoke with the old man, there was dead silence in the gathering that morning. True stillness is unusual with such a garrulous collection." He looked again at his suit. "All because of this three-piece suit of mine." He feigned cool. "Well, my landlord parades himself as a retired director in one of the Federal Ministries, but a proper profiling of his rise shows he was never on the payroll of that ministry for a day even as an office assistant ." He revealed to the audience

Then he folded his fist and threw some jabs into the air with usual animation..

"Leave my house! Leave my house!! He shouted. "The man became a pugilist eventually". He shook the podium. "But I did nothing because where I come from; it is an abomination to raise your voice or hand against an elder. All that tradition allows you to do in such situation is persevere" He dropped his head like a man bludgeoned on every side from a mass mob action, then moved back to the rightful position as is expected of such an official presentation.

"Ladies and Gentlemen." He looked up.

"Transformation is not at all a mouthy thing. Every human must know and perform their responsibility with mutual respect; shedding all togas of selfishness; leaving out any form of mistrust that may have come from any sick upbringing that is inherent in our systems, cultures and ideologies. We need to unlearn many of our animalistic orientations so we can have a real sense of humanness." He sounded philosophical. "No matter how plain a truth you present to a cheat ,he will only see mischief because his DNA is wired to lie". He stopped.

The wow of the audience can never be quantified, as

they stood with a resounding round of applause to express their great admiration of an enigma.

He stepped aside and took a bow.

When Kibela woke up, he was still in the suburb of Maputo.

TRIUMPHANT ISLAND

"**Judith**, quickly set the table for me," Josh said to his wife with no recourse to any amplitude of gratitude.

His friends, Benji and Stan, had come to visit him on this special occasion because he has just been appointed as the new Senior Special Adviser on People Living with Disabilities to the State Governor. They were awed at Josh's commandership even on his home front. They had thought his domineering personality would have abated as he advanced in age. They felt intimidated around him at all times because of his towering achievements, even though they stood on their two feet, a luxury he could not enjoy. The last time they saw him was at their third Reunion Party which was about a decade ago.

As Judith brought the food to the table his friends asked him how he came about such a belle for a wife. He laughed and hinted them on how he was determined to get not just a lady to wife, but a woman who would melt the heart of so many people who came in contact with her, men and women alike.

Judith was of the Tiv stock of the Middle-belt region of Nigeria. She was the daughter of the head of Lutheranism in Benue State. A Chartered Accountant by profession, she was well built and of moderate height. The radiant flux around her was indescribable.

Stan was so inquisitive about how Josh caught the fancy of Judith.

"What you able-bodied men do lack, we who are physically-challenged have in abundance," Josh said jokingly.

Josh had suffered Spinal Poliomyelitis at a very

tender age, resulting in the paralysis of his legs. Polio has killed and crippled thousands of children. This dreaded disease has caused so much harm that one would have thought it would have become a thing of the past, especially with great awareness and enlightenment campaigns being embarked upon by different organizations. But far from it; we still have victims of this disease, though minimal. Josh is not exempted from this minute data.

Josh grew to know himself as one who wears an Orthopedic Brace and ankle foot Orthotic. His parents appeared enlightened though they couldn't explain how he came to that state. He mastered it so well that he thought never could any other means of walking be more convenient: a quokka-like fellow.

The bulk of his confidence came from his upbringing as his parents never treated him as being different from any of their other children. They shared chores among them equally according to their age, and he being the first child took the responsibility of looking after his younger siblings, a task he thrived at tremendously.

Stan did a quick appraisal of his life. He is able bodied. Tall. Handsome. All his attempts at securing a lady of his dream had not paid off at all. He had tried his hands on quite a number. They either stopped seeing him after few outings or walked away at the beckon of a marriage possibility. He searched through himself, yet he found nothing wrong with his person. In addition, he had few currency notes to throw around. What could be wrong?

"Guys let's go do justice to this table as we jointly sacrifice to Limos, god of hunger." Josh invited his friends over as he stood up with the support of his walking stick. He used the stick at home, just as any man would pull off his jacket and change into something relaxing when he got back home from the day's work. Stan jerked back to consciousness and he joined the others in walking to the table. But deep down inside of him he had thought Josh would never get married with his condition and if at all he did, it would not be to a beautiful woman; but on seeing Judith, his resentment of Josh brewed again.

They practically grew up together in the same neighborhood, attended the same elementary and secondary schools, even the same university. The trio. Very good friends they had been and still are. The only time they were not in the same class was in the university, when they chose to study different courses, but all within the Faculty of Sciences.

Josh studied Physics and Mathematics. He graduated top of his class. One would have thought the goodwill he enjoyed from people would be due to his disability but far from it. He has a very amiable personality in addition to his intelligence. Anyone would only show great admiration for a determined individual who does not allow his predicament to hamper him from reaching his goal. He has at many times refused to be helped to move ahead in his walk and in his career, especially when he is climbing the stairs. He had been like that from his secondary school days. He was disgusted at the pity he was shown attending an elementary school. His teachers showed extra-ordinary care while tending to him, but he could not stop them because he was just getting out of his parent's domain to experiencing a new life, socializing with others. So, he took their gestures kindly, but hated to be pitied. Though brilliant, he felt he should be treated in opaque reality far away from his disability, the same way other kids were treated. Nobody should treat him in a special manner: every child, man, woman, able or physically-challenged, have equal rights. More so, he was just suffering from polio not dementia praecox. He objected to his parents' plan of sending him to a special secondary school for children with disabilities; they felt that as he grew older his challenges would increase.

Benji and Stan understood his challenge before they

got into the same school. He would watch them as they sprinted and played football in the neighborhood. Sometimes, he would devalue his physicality by choosing to join in the race but the other kids would give him a consideration as they allowed him to stay a meter to the finish line, so that he would end up being the winner: such races were for fun. When they attended the same school they would also help with his back pack even when he chose to carry it himself. They tended to him, and protected him from calumniators as well. They were big and fit enough to stand whatever pressure the challenge of any new environment may have posed. They were usually the bullies.

Josh was very good with algorithm and he usually helped his friends and classmates with their knotty mathematic equations. They would wonder how such an incapacitated lad was capable of such overt ingenuity. He knew that it was not from the crowd, nor the shouts or plaudits of the multitude, but right on the inside of him laid triumph or defeat, thus he chose the path of knowledge to ascertain his ability.

Again, he was loved by the teachers, but more for his intelligence.

While the dinner lasted, a little catching up was done.

"Immediately after I finished serving the government for the mandatory one year National Youth Service Corp, I got a job as an Insurance Sales Executive," Benji hinted.

"I worked that job for two years until I moved to another insurance company and I was made Assistant Sales Manager," Benji continued as he shared his career history with his friends and they listened. In between, Judith came in."If there is anything extra you want. Kindly let me know." She said as her face beamed with smiles as expected of a good host.

"This is our house Madame; we'll sure let you know," Benji and Stan chorused. "Thank you." they added.

Judith walked back inside with bowls of water for the

men used to wash their hands after the meal. As she walked away, Stan's eyes were still fixated on her-apodyopsis, until she went oblivious from the scene. As Stan turned his head in order to continue conversing with his friends his eyes met with disdain from Benji while Josh looked at him with a patronizing smile.

"Do you like her?" Josh bailed him out.

"She is your wife," He interjected.

"I can hands off for you if you want." He continued "You know I'll always do that for you." He added.

Josh and Stan were subjects of a scandal in their university days. Josh was involved with a sophomore while he was in the last year of his study. They both were so into one another and had the hope of taking it beyond the university walls if things worked to their best. The lady was in the same Department of Microbiology with Stan. Josh had grown so popular in school that the whole university community knew him to be the student with the overall highest CGPA in the school. So many people were always stunned when they finally met him. One would have wondered if they had taken a physically-challenged person for a dumbass. Barb and Josh became an inseparable couple in the university.

The jealousy of Stan was established as he made an amoral overture on Barb by being exceptionally kind to her on many occasions with suggestive intentions. As typical as it is of some women, they hardly can handle such gestures. She fell for him and he took her in. They started sleeping together. He started giving her what Josh was not. He had always wanted what Josh had.

Unfaithfulness can never be hidden forever, especially when a friend is hitting on his friend's girlfriend. Not long, the inculpation was confirmed and the whole university became keenly interested with the news of such a debauchery. Campus news boards were agog with the pictures and the gist of the escapades. It was a great betrayal by a friend.

The infraction between the two friends was later settled by their parents as they termed the girl to be lacking 'gemütlich' as the Germans will put it. But, all in all, Stan became infamous for this ingratiation, both at school and at home.

"He is the guy who snatched his friend's girlfriend." That was a singsong on many lips at the sighting of Stan in the neighborhood and on the campus. He appeared unperturbed by the comments as he was satisfied by taking away from Josh what he felt he was not entitled to. The same way any schizophrenic would behave.

The room became odoriferous and infested with the botheration Stan was grossly emitting through his insensibility.

As soon as they finished their meal, Benji skillfully suggested they should go to a recreation point somewhere close, so that they could really catch up on old times.

Josh beckoned at one of his attendants who quickly ran to his side and crouched to hear the instruction from his boss who spoke into his right ear. He walked out as soon as his boss finished talking.

While they were still talking, a white high-end vehicle came into the compound and pulled over right at the entrance of the duplex where they stood to have a chat. That signaled it was time to let them go. It was then they realized that Stan had not been standing with them. He was still inside the house. Benji ran into the house and yelled out at Stan to tell him it was time to go.

Josh was already seated in the vehicle and they joined him.

As the chauffeur got to a zebra crossing close to a shopping mall, he stopped for the pedestrians to cross to the other side of the road. There was another motorist, honking so stern behind them, threatening that their vehicle gives way so that he could drive on even though there were pedestrians crossing. Not many drivers and even the pedestrians themselves understood the road signs. The zebra crossing for example, typically painted in alternating black and white stripes on the road, is purposely made to give rights of way to pedestrians. But motorists often than not ignore the rule that states that once a pedestrian steps on the first white stripe of the zebra crossing sign, the motorist should stop for the pedestrian to cross before moving on.

"Do you know how I got this job?" Josh was ready to tell his friends how the governor appointed him as his advisor.

It was one hot afternoon, on his way to a client's office that he witnessed a fatal accident. It involved a Bullion Van conveying God knows what and a blind person who had his white cane with him. He was already lying lifeless on the road in his own blood. Common sense would have pointed that whoever, whenever, and wherever, one sees a white cane it suggests that the holder is visually impaired and should be possibly be helped, but in this clime not so many people have that sense of common knowledge. Rather, many motorists have gone ahead to knock down, and in many cases run over such individuals; even pedestrians show no courtesy or assistance to such impaired people. Just because a person is visually impaired does not mean that he or she should not move about.

Josh had to get out of his car to stand right in front of the van, as the driver and the police officers in it tried to find a leeway, to escape the scene as is typical of trigger-happy police men. He stood his ground at the risk of his life. Ordinarily, he would have been killed on the grounds that he was trying to hijack the funds in the van if not for the fortunate arrival of the governor's convoy that was on its way to an occasion. The Governor had to be forced to come out of his vehicle due to the *autoschlange* -- long traffic that was very unusual on that particular road. The Governor, who led by example, instructed his aides and officers not to blare sirens in the state, as characterized by other politicians and office holders in the country. Public office holders are expected to uphold the law to the minutest of it, but they are usually the ones who would drive against the traffic rules. Many times, they have killed people in that insanity.

The Governor had to order that the bullion van and its occupants be detained, while he consoled Josh who was soaked in his own sweat and tears. The governor was kind to comfort Josh, who had seen the body of a human mangled on the surface of the road like a fly that was hit by a fifty kilogram sledge hammer. More so, he shared the same affection. He was also a person with disability.

The Governor gave him his contacts and encouraged Josh to call him.

A few days after the accident, the governor invited him to the State House and commended his courage to stand right for justice. Had it not been for Josh, the killer driver would have bolted. So many people would not come out to stand as witnesses in such a case, which inadvertently makes inquests to such killings fruitless.

He presented a SWOT Matrix of the governor in a friable way that no one has ever done, and also a blueprint of steps that the government could take to ameliorate the hardship that society imposed on people living with disability.

Many evolving societies build high rise structures with no provision for people who may need aid to get to different floors of the building. They build roads with no provisions for pedestrians, not to mention purvey for the physically-challenged. Segregation of the physically-challenged from the "able-bodied" in opportunity accessibility like employment ,is a case in point in many places. Legislation proviso should be adequate to include people with disability of any form.

The governor appreciated Josh's effort especially with his SWOT analysis. Anyway, it is expected that if a man is hungry he should do something positive to kill his hunger. So also, if we want a change we should stand right for the change we so demand. Not just talk. Act.

The Governor saw a good brain that could contribute immensely to the advancement of the state, and he invited him to serve the people under his government. He was appointed one of the governor's aides.

"That is how I became the Special Adviser." Josh ended his narration.

Mostly, his friends were taken aback at his undying courage as they always found him to be courageous. He participated in Student Unionism in their university days. He was at the forefront of every struggle to improve the living conditions of students. He also fought the school authority each time they tried to increase the tuition. People who knew him in the university respected him for his piquant quality in articulating common views of the studentry, that on so many occasions his own oration geared the students to take action and to resist any oppression under whatsoever guise. Activism was part of him.

As they got to the golf course, the chauffeur opened the door of the car and Josh was greeted by other golfers. A caddie ran to them and retrieved Josh's bag from the car boot.

"This is a game of the elites," Stan said as a golf cart came to convey them to the putting green. As the cart lurched, Josh changed his shoes. Of course, he had a special pair of shoes, not the common spike shoes. He is an uncommon being and deserves uncommon things.

Benji was also thrilled at the height that their friend had arrived. Some whatchamacallits were just dropping freely from his lips too. This was their first entrance into a golf course as they believed that playing golf was for the super-rich.

"Golf is expensive no doubt but it is not for a particular set of people," Josh corrected them.

As they alighted from the cart, a very beautiful lady waved at Josh and he returned her greeting.

Benji asked Josh, "Is she a member of the golf club too?"

"Yes, so many of them," Josh answered.

"That means I may have to come with you often," he said with a delighted smile on his face. They laughed.

Stan easily lost himself at the sight of a pretty lady. Curse-laden. He was pulled at his shirt by Benji as another lady strolled toward them.

"Hello gentlemen," the lady said with her arms stretched to hug Josh, and in turn she shook hands with Benji and Stan.

"Let me do the honor." Josh tried to do the introduction. "Stan and Benji," he added. "My good friends and school mates from way back." He ended the warm introduction.

She was one of Josh's numerous exes, rich, flamboyant, and single. She didn't mind being a second wife to Josh. She just wanted him. One would have submitted: what could a pretty lady of that calibre have wanted with a married, polio-infested man like Josh? But, what makes a man is not his physique; he may be neat and decent looking, what is in his heart matters more. Josh has a good heart and so many frills attached thereto.

As expected, Stan wandered away 'round the course, but not for long. He settled to a seat close to a lady golfer and they engaged one another in a chat. That left Josh and Benji an ample amount of time to have a real chat.

"I am sorry for what Stan did at your house," Benji broke the silence.

"It is nothing. I have always known him from the university." He shrugged his apology off.

"So tell me what brought you around?" He probed.

"Nothing much my dear friend. Apart from going to see the newest Special Assistant in town." They laughed at the sound of that. "Actually, we came because of Stan," he hinted.

Josh demanded, "What about him?"

He finally submitted, "He has been without a job for a long time now, and we came because we know you will need people to work with you."

A Quick scenery ran through Josh's mind. Ten years ago...

About a decade ago when he last saw his friends at their third reunion, Josh determined he would not attend the reunion again or be at any place where he would not be respected, especially amongst his peers. His reason was that he had gone there without a car, and had not bought one since then. Stan was there with his car; likewise did Benji. Since Stan was living close to him at that particular time, Josh made an arrangement to ride with him. But in spite of their agreement, Stan had given an excuse that he was not going for the Reunion Party which left Josh with no option than to go by public transport to the venue, only to find Stan at the party in company of Barbra. He felt so disgusted due to the malefic done him by someone he called a friend. But, because of his happy nature, he overlooked that behavior, and even went to greet the duo of Stan and Barb, only to be ignored totally by them. That was the last time he set his eyes on him before Stan and Benji showed up in his house that morning.

As he raised his head he smiled with deep peace oozing from the depth of his heart.

"Do you think this guy is ready to change at all?" he inquired from Benji, as they both looked at the direction of Stan who was busy chatting away his new acquaintance. He was like a man who had gone to borrow a garb but gormandized away his purpose, when offered a feast. Someone more serious and not distracted came and got the garb instead.

"No matter what, he is still a brother. He may not be a good friend, but what can we do." Benji tried to convince Josh. "He has been living off me for some time now," he chipped in.

Now it became clearer to Josh why Benji advocated for him. He wanted to get him off his back.

Josh said, "I am still in ideation stage now, as you are well aware that my office has just been newly created. As soon as I am seeking officers to work with me I will let you know," he added as he handed his Calling Card to Benji to give it to Stan. "He will only meet me in the office not my house," he doled out emphatically as they both smiled.

Josh sought to bring on board to work with him, people who had strong affection for and with people living with disabilities. Autism, deaf, mute, visual impairment, lames, and the likes are some of the challenges he would look into and would advise the Governor on, most appropriately. So he had not seen how Stan fit into any of these parameters. Maybe he would have him seconded to another advisor in the ministry of women affairs.

A call came through for Josh to come over to the house where his siblings were waiting for him. He immediately informed his friends that he had to go home. He said that he would be willing to drop them off if they were ready to go, or else they could stay back and have their fun. To the latter they subscribed, since they could navigate their way to their destination with the help of a cab. He bade them farewell as they walked him to the car.

Judith and Josh's siblings were chatting away as she already informed them of the happenstance before their arrival. Once he came in, his siblings asked if it was who they thought had come to the house, and he confirmed their curiosity. They burst into laughter; everybody, including his wife.

"A chameleon will always be a chameleon," one of them submitted; they laughed the more.

Barb's marital status on Facebook has been reading "complicated" for a record time now…

ZIP CODE

Having completed my internship, I was posted to Ifesowapo for my mandatory one- year National Youth Service Corp programme. It is a bubbly village; lively people. I had opted to serve in the deepest of the hinterland so as to offer myself for service in the true sense of it. The people of Ifesowapo hardly get a Youth 'Corper' to serve in their domain, so I was welcomed into their midst like a Royal. In fact, I was given a room in the King's cottage; of course, at no cost and with other benefits.

As time went by, the people of Ifesowapo became more and more relaxed with me and vice versa. The King would sometimes invite me for a chat with him. On this particular day, the king called me into his inner chamber as usual, but this time he wanted to share a secret with me.
"My son, Prince Omogoriola, lives in the city with his wife and kids." The king started out. "But before he left this town, he had put one of our maids in the family way. In fact, that was one reason his journey to the city was fast-tracked, as it is a shameful thing for the royals to share intimacy with the dregs".

At the sound of the word dregs, I chuckled, because in my few months in the village, everyone lived together in harmony, just as the name suggests; but that morning, I learnt that the wind that is blowing everywhere also breezes here. I am used to city life where it is everyman for himself, and if at all you get to be made part of a team, it will come based on one or more colorations that you bear; not on one's ingenuity, capacity and or capability. That was the main reason I chose the deepest of the hinterland for my youth service.

During the 3week Orientation and camping period, the Commandant had hinted that the state was dearth of Medical Doctors; hence, we may be drafted to work at the State House Hospital. It took me extra effort to convince the officers at the State secretariat of the National Youth Service Corps to have me redeployed to a village. They purposely chose Ifesowapo because they believed I will be frustrated and will eventually rush back to them to be redeployed back to the city.

Ifesowapo is a village that has no power supply, whose drinking water comes from a manually operated tap that exhausts one's energy in operating, but in the real sense, one gets to burn some calories. I was not allowed to operate it for once anyway; I told you I was treated like a royal.

"After Omogoriola left, we tried sending the maid to her village because she had come here on servitude-for-loan agreement, but we had to release her to cover our shame." The king continued. "I blessed her with gifts and in the company of escorts who helped her with her luggage, she fell into labor on the way to her village. The escorts came back with a set of twins, two handsome boys. When I asked for the mother, they told me she passed while in labor because there was no Iya Abiye to attend to her." The king bowed his head, obviously remorseful for taking such a send-her-away decision.

"Where are the twins?" I asked.

The king of Ifesowapo, the Olori Omoogun, on whose order the village is brought to her knees, the man with much agility and burning passion that lights up the firewood without a matchstick, looked up with teary eyes and said "my grandsons are locked up in a room, both of them".

I probed to know what could have earned them imprisonment in the land of their forebears. What?

"I think the gods decided to punish me for the cruel choice I made concerning their mother", he submitted.

"They were struck by strange ailments. One shakes his head uncontrollably, drowning himself in his own spittle, and the other does not just want to talk to anybody, acting strangely such that he just looks at you and says nothing even though they are in their late twenties". He bowed his head again.

It was just both of us in the room except for our shadows on the wall. I wonder why he would be so free to take me into confidence, as he revealed that no one sees the twins except their caregivers who have been sternly warned through the thunder threat of the impassionate kingdom head.

"Those are my grandsons. The only ones I have as Omogoriola has not come back to the village again neither can anyone except Goriola or his sons mount this throne of my forefathers. I am in a fix." The king is now confused. "I pray the gods dissolve their conspiracy against me". His belief.

"Kabiesi, can I get to see them?" I said that still displaying my unshaken obeisance to the king.

He raised his kingly head this time, looked at me straightly. The Sauline assessment of David's teen.

I nodded, signaling a reassurance that I would want to do this.

"What do you think you can do?" He inquired.

I know these people hardly have access to medical services, not to mention the knowledge needed to treat many minor cases that even an ORT would have sorted expressly. At the same time, I was cautious of friction that may emanate with the Herb Consultants Association in Ifesowapo.

"Let me see them first Your Highness!" I retorted.

"Come with me". He came down from his throne in the inner chamber, led the way and I followed.

He is sure a man with much agility, even in his advanced age. He shows much dexterity of the mapping of the cottage, as is expected of a man who has lived his life all around the palace, full of wits. He ordered that a particular door, that seemingly zip-coded his two grandsons, be opened. To my stern gaze, I could tell Down and Asperger Syndromes. Both are manageable. It is not the gods.

As I made to utter a statement, my mind sunk into a reverie:

One of those moments in the medical college when we got attached to a specialist so that we can get a hands-on experience while we also learn from the Masters. I chose paediatrics .

A certain man not too deep into his midlife, had come into the children's ward with his baby who was about twenty-four months old. He complained about the unusual behavior being exhibited by his daughter. He wanted an evaluation of the beautiful baby. "His angel" as he referred to her many times in his communication.

"I noticed, my angel doesn't make any facial expression of any kind." The man answered when the doctor queried to know some of the signs the toddler was showing.

"Was there any vocal expression at anytime like blabbing?" The doc queried further.

" Not a single one", the man responded as he cleaned the pretty young girl as she burped. He smiled at her, expectant that she would respond

There is an index of Autism Spectrum Disorders(ASD) but the paeditrician didn't want to make any hurried decision.

"We would have to bring in some other specialists on board so as to be able to draw an informed conclusion." The doctor informed the father of the toddler.

Without blinking, the father submitted that they should be brought in, in fact, he wanted it done straight away but due to very high demand on the few doctors in those fields, they may have to be booked.

"I'm sorry Mr Omoboriowo, it's not that easy. We may have to inform these experts and get appointments", the pediatrician informed him and a fatal deflation of his anxiety could be told., "we will inform you of the appointments", the doc concluded.

"Appointments?", the man asked.

"Yes, you will have to see a psychologist, speech and language therapists, as well as an occupational therapist. A comprehensive laboratory examination needs to be carried out for us to understand the situation we have at hand. " The doctor briefly counseled the young father; but in all, much encouragement was given to Mr. Omoboriowo . He walked out of the clinic, a hopeful man.

I engaged my teacher in a chat after the day's work. I was so keen on knowing more about the possibility of Mr. Omoboriowo not losing or regaining hope in the bid of having his angel active. Mr Omoboriowo had hinted that he is a widower.

"Mr Omoboriowo's daughter is suffering from Asperger syndrome", my teacher pointed to me and that is a new one for me.

It was an assignment for me.

****

Asperger syndrome, also called Asperger disorder, is a type of pervasive developmental disorder (PDD). PDDs are a group of conditions that involves delay in the development of basic skills, notably the ability to socialize with others, to communicate, and to use one's imagination.

Although Asperger syndrome is similar in some ways to autism -- another, more severe type of PDD -- there are some important differences. Children with Asperger syndrome typically function better than do those with autism. In addition, children with Asperger syndrome generally have normal intelligence and near-normal language development, although they may develop problems communicating as they get older.

Asperger syndrome has only recently been recognized as a unique disorder. For that reason, the exact number of people with the disorder is unknown. While it is more common than autism, it is four times more likely to occur in males than in females and usually is first diagnosed in children between the ages of two and six years. The exact cause of Asperger syndrome is not known. However, the fact that it tends to run in families suggests that a tendency to develop the disorder may be inherited (passed on from parent to child).

The symptoms of Asperger syndrome vary and can range from mild to severe. Common symptoms include:

Problems with social skills like having difficulty interacting with others. Sufferers are often awkward in social situations. They generally do not make friends easily. They have difficulty initiating and maintaining conversations;

Eccentric or repetitive behaviors by developing odd, repetitive movements, such as hand wringing or finger twisting;
Unusual preoccupations or rituals such as getting dressed in a particular order;

Communication difficulties like not making eye contact when speaking with someone. They may have trouble using facial expressions and gestures, and understanding body language. They also tend to have problems understanding language in context and are very literal in their use of language;

Limited range of interests like developing an intense, almost obsessive interest in a few areas, such as sports schedules, weather, or maps;

Coordination problems by being clumsy.

Down syndrome also known as trisomy 21, is caused by a gene problem that happens before birth. Children who have Down syndrome tend to have certain features, such as a flat face and a short neck. They also have some degree of intellectual disability. This varies from person to person. But in most cases it is mild to moderate.

Down syndrome is caused by a problem with a baby's chromosomes. Normally, a person has 46 chromosomes. But most people with Down syndrome have 47 chromosomes. In rare cases, other chromosome problems cause Down syndrome. Having extra or abnormal chromosomes changes the way the brain and body develop.

Experts do not know the exact cause, but some things increase the chance that you will have a baby with Down syndrome. These things are called risk factors:

You are older when you get pregnant. Many doctors believe that the risk increases for women age 35 and older or if you have a brother or sister who has Down syndrome.

Most children with Down syndrome have:

Distinctive facial features, such as a flat face, small ears, slanting eyes, and a small mouth;

A short neck and short arms and legs;

Weak muscles and loose joints. Muscle tone usually improves by late childhood;

Below-average intelligence.

Many children with Down syndrome are also born with heart, intestine, ear, or breathing problems.

These health conditions often lead to other problems, such as airway (respiratory) infections or hearing loss. But most of these problems can be treated.

A doctor may suggest that you have tests during pregnancy to find out if your baby has Down syndrome. You may decide to have:

Screening tests, such as an ultrasound or a blood test during your first or second trimester. These can help show if the developing baby (fetus) is at risk for Down syndrome. But these tests sometimes give false-positive or false-negative results.

Diagnostic tests, such as chorionic villus sampling or amniocentesis. These can show if a baby has Down syndrome. You may want to have these tests if you have abnormal results from a screening test or if you are worried about Down syndrome.

Sometimes a baby is diagnosed after birth. A doctor may have a good idea that a baby has Down syndrome based on the way the baby looks and the results of a physical exam. To make sure, the baby's blood will be tested.

Credit: WebMD.com

Mr Omoboriowo came back few days later after completing his rounds of appointment. Though he looked helpless, but highly hopeful that he is not going to lose his daughter to any form of ailment.

In the course of his meetings, he has been enlightened that most importantly these children could be exceptionally talented and have unique skills. Downs and Asperger syndromes are lifelong conditions. But with care and support, most children who have them can grow up to live healthy, happy, productive lives.

****

This story was inspired by a friend, whose two boys have Downs and Asperger Syndromes respectively. She cares for both of them all night and day. She is a nurse. A very strong woman.

Ebi Anthony

Born on April 26, 1996, Bayelsa State, Nigeria. She lives with her grandmother in Lagos, having been separated from her parents at the age of nine. She is the fourth of numerous other children from her parents.

"I do not have pleasant childhood memories. I grew up without parental love as I didn't have the opportunity to grow up in a family setting. My father is a polygamist and having to survive was difficult for us all. After three years of staying with my grandmother, I had the chance to study for primary and secondary education with the assistance of an uncle."

Ebi does menial jobs to support herself, her grandmother and even sends money home to her dear mother. She currently works as a SIM Registration Agent on contract basis for one of the telcos in Nigeria. She wants to study Mass Communication or English Language someday and become a writer.

Tears of A Woman is her first.

TEARS OF A WOMAN

Earth was a paradise for me, I knew no pain as my parents showed me great love. Life was a place of comfort for me, everything was great, the love between father and mother was peerless. The love between the duo became more intense when mother got pregnant again. Father made life more comfortable for her and she could be taken as the luckiest woman on earth. Mother visited the doctor for her routine checks. The imagination of having a younger sibling made me so happy; we will tell each other how much we adore our parents; I could assist with his assignment when he is old enough to start school. But like a broken egg that cannot be fixed again, the world I knew as a child crumbled before my eyes when things started changing at home. Father, who was a loving husband, became a monster. He turned mother into a punching bag, making life a living hell for her. Heavy pains engulfed me to see the home tearing apart.

Mother has not checked the sex of the baby but we generally believed it would be a boy. I felt it whenever am around her; the coming baby will be a joy that will fill her empty heart, a heart that has been longing to bear another child. The pressure from her in-laws would get so unbearable at times that she would break down and weep bitterly to the point of saturation. Father had been pleaded with several times to get another wife, but he would not bulge as he turned deaf ears to such counsel by his parents.

"Your wife, Dorcas is a bad woman. Her wayward life has caught up with her, if you continue to live with this woman, you will die a father of one child" This was always ringed to his ears by Mama Wakore, my grandmother.

Father showed love to mother despite the many pressures from his parents and friends.

One night, I heard a grieving shout and I ran to mother's room to find her in a pool of her own blood.

"Mother!" I shouted with a shaky voice. She tried to speak but streams of tears wouldn't let her. I held her up to get her off the floor; I reached for the door handle trembling as I led her to the car outside. I took Mary, the househelp with me, and the driver drove us to the hospital.

About an hour later, father rushed down to the hospital, having been informed of his wife's condition. He came breathing like a person who had just completed a four-hundred metre race, and went straight to the doctor's office. Few minutes later, he came out with a sad face. I moved closer to him and gave him a hug. I felt his pulsating heart beating faster than normal; his eyes moved from side to side and I wondered what could be running through his mind.

Back home, the thought of mother in the hospital made me an insomniac for the rest of the night and my eyes became swollen from weeping. I suddenly became nostalgic of mother's gentle touch and her soft kisses; she would always come to my room in the night to give me soft kisses and say "good night".

When in the wake of the day, I was finally able to close my eyes in sleep, I found myself in a different world, a world which came only in sleep.

I walked through a path which was totally strange to my eyes; blood stains all over the wall and the cry of a baby rent the air. I was unable to locate the crying baby no matter how hard I followed the cries. Suddenly, I felt a cold hand around me.

"Father", I called out and I rested by head on his bosom. He cut short the mysterious dream I was having as he woke me.

"Everything will be fine." He assured me in a low tone.

Mrs. Johnson noticed that I have not been in my usual elements as I couldn't concentrate in school for the next few days.

"What is bothering you my dear?", she inquired even when she knew me to be a gentle girl. I wanted to talk that mother was rushed to the hospital, but I said nothing. No matter how much she probed into my worry- filled eyes, nothing came out of my mouth.

After school hours, the driver drove me to the hospital where I found mother lying helplessly on the bed. I held her hand as she made efforts to sit up.

"How was school?", she said with a fainting voice.

"School was fine." I replied.

"Did Mary cook according to the food table made for you?"

"Yes"

She tried to say some nice things but I placed my hands to her lips to prevent her from saying any other word. She moved her lips close to my ear, and whispered a word; I looked into her face to figure what she was trying to tell me but it was dead blank.

I was in my room studying on a sunny Saturday when I heard a knock on my door. It was Mary at the front door.

"Madam! Madam!!" She shouted welcoming mother back home.

I dashed out of my room to meet mother. She looked sad and her lips were white as if a heavy harmattan has fed on them. She was looking older than her age. Her unkempt hair stood like dry grasses that are waiting to be showered by rains. She had become visibly emaciated these past four days she had spent in the hospital and I helped her to her room.

"Does it mean what happened to her sucked her youthful look?" I wondered.

As I stood to leave her room to meet father, she called me by my traditional name "Oyindinepre", with a melancholic voice. I stopped to look at her.

"Mother", I responded and I moved closer to her.

"I lost the baby", she said amidst heavy weeping.

I stood there like a person who has been hit by a heavy stone. I became transfixed at that spot; statute still.

"Is this a dream?" I closed my eyes to make myself believe that all these are nothing but a dream.

I was brought back to the real world, when my father shouted my name again with a voice that is more thunderous tone than the last one I heard. It was not a dream and the truth stood right before me. Mother's miscarriage brought pain to my heart and caused it to bleed severely. Father came to mother's room after a long wait for me.

"Oyindinepre!" Father shouted my name once more.

"Did you not hear me call you?"

I tried to tell father how sorry I was.

"Mother lost her baby" were the words that came out of my mouth. Father stared at me for a while and came closer to hold me in his arms. He said we can't change what has happened and life has to move on.

In the first week of the eleventh month after losing her baby, mother decided to surrender everything to God and asked God to reward her womb again. She decided to visit Mama Ebeleye.

Mama Ebeleye is a loving grandma, who has loved and supported her daughter all the way. She often told mother to be strong, for she will be fruitful as she bore seven children for her husband. My maternal grandma, who wanted to save her daughter's marriage suggested that mother see a powerful man of God who she believed can see what physical eyes cannot see. Mother doesn't give ear to such talk.

"Mama, these prophets cannot solve my problem, they will only compound it. They are pocket eaters. Don't bother yourself I know God will reward me"

Mama Ebeleye would not listen to her daughter; she insisted mother should see the prophet who can find a solution to her misfortunes.

"Mama, I don't want to see them" said mother in more convincing manner.

"Don't you want another child? Heed my voice my daughter and act fast before your husband kicks you out like a common thief." The stern desperation of mama urging her daughter to go through fetish means to solve her problems was amazing

"Mama Ebimobowei can't do that to me".

This time mama was louder than before, "don't come running to me when your husband kicks you out."

Mother looked at her motionlessly, "why mama, don't you want to accept the fact that only God gives children?"

She came back from the village a week later.

Father who had been a loving husband wore a new colour and pounced on mother.

"Where are you coming from?", father asked in a demanding voice.

"Ebimobowei, my husband, what went wrong?" mother asked,.

"Everything!", father replied.

"But I told you I was going to visit mama and you gave me the permission to go."

"I did not ask you to go", father's had reached the highest pitch.

I went to my room to keep myself busy in order to avoid unnecessary talks from my father. While reading, I heard a violent sound that is suggestive of beating from down stairs and uncontrollable fear gripped me. I stood at the entrance of the living room to see what was happening.

"You slapped me?" mother said in a low voice

"Yes and I will do it again if you do not tell me where you are coming from."

"You don't trust me after all these years we have been together?"

"Ebimobowei, what have I done to you to deserve all these from you?" The soft words pushed dad to his room leaving mother helpless and uncared for.

"Why did he do this to me?" she sobbed the more as she continued her monologue.

I went to mother's room to see if she was okay but to my surprise I saw a dark mark had formed on her right cheek close to her eye; the spot looked like roasted corn which had been left too long on the burner.

"Are you alright Mother?" I wanted to ask her if it hurt but the right words refused to come; instead other words found their way out. I knew she was not in good shape. She moved her hands to mine and said "Oyin, do not hate your father despite his beastly behavior".

I couldn't understand why mother asked me not to hate father when the thought of hating father never came to my mind: a good father and a loving husband, a man of integrity. Though the mystery behind father's rash behavior got me worried, there is no place in my heart for hating father.

"Why did he raise his hand to hit mother?" I tried to fathom a meaningful explanation for father's actions but nothing came up. The breeze of the love father and mother shared came rushing at my head like a heavy wave. The love they shared was rare . Neighbours envied them to the point that mother was accused of charming father; but father was not under any enchantment, theirs was a marriage ordained by God.

The scar in his heart was too big to be healed.
"The joy of any marriage is the reward of the womb", as Papa Waredwei, his father, my grandpa would tell him." A man cannot be called a real man until children succeed him".

We all listened to Reverend Paul quote the scriptures when he majestically mounted the altar to preach. I thought about how many times we have not been regular in church due to the changes that had taken place at home. I heard Reverend Paul say "it is good to give" in a loud voice. "A cheerful giver will not lack." Although the congregation was as silent as a grave yard, he would still shout.

Reverend Paul is a young man of an average height, the new parish priest that just got transferred to St. Anglican Mission Church. Since he came, the doctrines of the church had changed. His pointed nose always looked down on the congregation whenever he is preaching. The major change was that Reverend Paul's sermons were based on prosperity: how God will bless His children, if they obey His commandments. The congregation would listen attentively to him each time he mounts the altar to preach. Whenever he shouts "God will bless you". a thunderous AMEN will resound amongst members of the congregation.

During Sunday school when members were given the opportunity, some will ask questions that are far from what was being taught. Majority of the members prefer Reverend Paul's sermons to Reverend Morris' who loved to preach about holiness and righteousness. The congregation sometimes get bored listening to Morris' sermons as his messages got them afraid; many rejoiced when Morris was transferred to another parish.

As we drove home from church, we listened to songs from the cassette we recently bought from the books and cd vendor in the church. I didn't really enjoy the music being played as my mind went back to the sermon that was preached in the church. I heard father asking mother if she enjoyed the service and in her usual voice she said "yes". Mothers' face was not as bright as I expected it to be. She looked troubled. The grey blouse she wore covered what was bothering her. Everyone in the car was silent except for the message coming from the cassette player and a few punctures of chats that were far between.

I ran to my room to change from my church dress into something more comfortable: I need to settle down to my lunch of fried rice and chicken. Traditionally, father prayed over the food and by the time he's done, the organs in my stomach were already making some loud noise to remind me they couldn't wait any longer. Lunch was served and I ate with so much relish I forgot about all the troubles around me for once. Lunch done, off I went to my room upstairs.

About twenty minutes later, a knock on the door of the living room jolted me from my nap. It was Mary's voice that followed:

"It is Papa and Mama!"

I ran downstairs to meet to meet my grandparents with great amazement. I jumped on my Grandma to give her a hug, sat n her laps and rested my head against her arm ,caressing it at the same time. Mama being so tired, asked Mary to give her a glass of water.

In my girlish innocence and with a lot of joy in my heart, I asked Mama why she hasn't visited us for a while.

"I'm sorry my daughter, I will visit more often now".

Father walked into the living room with mother and with broad smiles on their faces they sat opposite Mama and Papa. They talked for awhile, asking how the journey was, amidst other things that were necessary to talk about.

I was asked to go up to my room and allow Mama and Papa Warowei have a little rest after their long journey from Yenogoa

Later that evening, father and grandpa had a long discussion. Father's voice was low but became higher and higher as the discussion progressed. Papa Warowei's voice was at the basest. I stood at the kitchen door which was closer to the living room as I tried to make myself as invisible as possible: I wanted to know what made father's voice reach such loud crescendo; I must not be caught doing that!

"I can't do that."

I wondered what Papa told father for him to have raised his voice at him. The thought of father's action got me disturbed.

Was papa asking father to marry another woman? I thought

Grandparents Warowei barely stayed in our home as they left for the village the third morning. I was getting dressed for school when mother slowly walked into my room to inform me that my grandparents were leaving. I expected mother to be happy but with the expression on her face, she was not. Mama treated mother with a cruel disposition for those two days she spent in our house. I wondered if there was any other reason behind Mama's behaviour towards mother apart from mother's inability to bear her more grandchildren.. If there was any, what was it?

Mother couldn't react negatively due to the love and respect she has for mama. Mother is a gentle person who does not like involving herself in anything that will bring chaos trouble or acrimony. Whenever she is badly hurt, tears were our words.

Mama had demanded "give me more grandchildren" as if it was mother that hoarded the fruits of the womb. This drama at home made me so sad. Many times, I would talk to mother, put my arms around her to console her; telling her she is not alone as she has me at all times. I could not understand mother's mood about the hurried exit of her parents' in-law. The sorrow in her eyes would not permit me to.

"Mother, why this mood?" I finally found my voice. I looked at her face as she made my hair. I saw her eyes been brighten up by something I could tell was a little smile, which forced it way out and made her lips take a curved shape.

The Driver was already waiting for me in the car. I went to school with the thought of not coming back to see Papa and Mama in our house. Mother who usually stood at the door to welcome me home with a warm hug was not there as expected, but was sitting in one of the sofas in the living room; tired; the brightness

I saw in her eyes earlier in the day was still there. She asked Mary to help me with my bag and ordered me to come downstairs and have my lunch as soon as I change my dress.

"Oyin, why are you not eating?" Mother asked as she came to the dining room and found me fiddling with my spoon. In a very low voice, I answered "I'm not hungry." knowing that she will be worried about me.

She caressed my hair," Dulofi, eat a little at least", she said as she sat beside me to pet me into eating during which time father walked in and I ran to hug him. Dulofi is my parent's pet name for me.

"How was school?" father asked.

"Fine!" I replied.

Father went into his room without saying anything to mother. It is father's custom to carry his suit case by himself; he does not allow anyone to carry it. Mother went to ask him if he needed anything to be prepared for him. She came back few minutes later and asked Mary to boil water. I saw his entrance as my exit from the dining room; an escape from the meal. I went to my room to do my assignment and not quite long after, I heard the door to father's room open and I suspect it was mother going into her husband's room.

"I want to rest." These were the words from father's room; it came in a rather loud voice as he slammed his door shut to whoever wanted to go in there.

To hide her humiliation, mother came into my room to see if I was working on my assignment, she went through my notes to see what I was taught for the day. She oft encourage me to work hard and to avoid all form of distraction. In all, she didn't tell me why father shouted and why she suddenly looks sad. Father did not come downstairs for supper; Mother and I ate alone on the big dining table that was meant for a family of six. Mother's eyes were clouded with tears that dropped slowly, though she tried to force the tears back.

"Are you okay?"

"Yes, I am fine", she responded, "it is just a headache; please dear don't worry about me". I knew it was not just a headache that caused those tears, but something much more than that, which seems to be eating her up slowly from the inside.

Why is father not here with us? Why did he decide to stay back in his room? Questions begging for answers.

The next morning was a weekend and on weekends we usually have a nice family time; but this weekend was an exception. Unsolved mysteries had broken down the happy home I once knew. Things took a different dimension and our home began to crumble. Father refused to come downstairs from his room for family time.

The family times we used to have were great experiences. We would all engage one another in different games, doing a lot of things together and telling one another how much we love and adore the other person. But now, life is showing us its ugly side and Its so hard to bear. Mother went to his room to check on father and returned to tell me father was okay but only needed some rest due to stress. She spoke with me having a forced smile on her face.

I prayed that night that God would restore love, joy and peace to our home. Am an avid reader of the Bible so I believe that if a family is in trouble, they could call upon God and He shall restore their peace.

I woke up tired the next morning but I managed to stand on my feet; stretch my body and went back to bed. *"Your father dey call you!"* Mary had said in pidgin English as she gently touched me to come to life. For minutes, I laid there, half awake, looking at her. She repeated *"your father dey call you"*, this time I understood what she said and I rushed to father's room not realizing I was still in my night gown. Father was on his bed when i entered his room. He asked me to sit on his bed. I sat down expecting him to say something but instead he looked into my face. I broke the silence and asked if he was okay. He kept mute. The look on his face told me not to ask another question. About ten minutes later, he finally opened his mouth.

"Why are you still in your night gown?" "Are you not going to school?" a two- pronged question.

Suddenly I became conscious of what I was wearing. The night gown was silky, transparent and was showing the little nuts that were developing in my chest. Shyness overshadowed me. As I made to leave his room, father said he was travelling. I turned to look at him "when?" I blurted out.

"Today", he said still looking at me. I stood there speechless; words were not coming forth. He was going to miss me I can tell. The desire to hug father hooked me down heavily and I was unable to escape these burning desires. I want to feel those eyes before leaving his room. Why is he travelling? Why leaving mother and I behind? The unpleasant thought clouded my head and forced tears to run down my cheeks.

"Oyindinepre, my daughter, why shed tears?" his voice was full of love.

"Father, why are you travelling?" I said expecting answers from him. He made effort to stand and move closer to me. I hugged him without realizing it. I felt his beating heart and his warm body against mine, it felt so good. The sweetness of his warm body sent back the tears that as filled my eyes. Million questions rushed to my head but I found my courage was been melted away by father's hug. Still in his arms I heard mother called my name in her sweet voice. That moment I made a move to free myself from his hug to meet mother. Something forced its way out my mouth in a low whisper; words which I didn't know where they came from.

"I will miss you, father." He looked at me and whispered same word to me. Those words hit me emotionally and tears streamed down my cheeks without control.

"Don't go, father." Those were the words that came out with the tears before I left his room.

Back in school, I was sleeping with my head laid on my desk when Beauty, my classmate, woke me.

"Has the school closed?" She looked at me with suspicion and said "Yes, about ten minutes ago". I quickly picked my bag to leave when she inquired if I was alright.
"Yes, I am fine" . Without looking at her, I ran out to meet the driver who I believed would be waiting for me in the car. On getting home, I was surprised to see my father's car neatly parked in the compound. Joy enveloped me and I ran to father's room, without minding my steps on the staircase.

"Father!" I had called out hoping to see him in his room, and when I knocked there was no response; so i forced the door open but room was empty. I burst into tears and rolled on the floor at the same time.

"Oyin, don't cry, my daughter, he will be back. Please don't cry". Tears streamed down her own eyes as she pacified me. She held me tight to herself as we both cried our hearts out.

It was an unpleasant month for us. Since father left the house; life was not the same. I became lonelier.
Mrs. Anthony called all students to assemble for a brief discussion. Without delay, they assembled before her according to their classes.

"I want you all to listen to me attentively", she stated. "Unity High School!...", she took the lead and all students chorused "Unity stands forever."

"I hope all students are present in the assembly?" Suddenly, pupils looked from side to side to see if any student was absent.

"I called this assembly to address all of you about this thing called 'Date Affair' in the school. It has come to my notice that many of you are involved in the said phenomenon. Do you know what it takes to date? It involves a relationship with the opposite sex, but I don't think you all know what it takes because If you do, I would not receive reports of messy stuff that occur in the school in the name of dating" Mrs. Anthony continued her talk. The noise from the students increased more and more.

"Everyone, keep quiet and listen to me", she commandeered. "I know those of you that are involved in this date affair in the school but am not here to call names. I only want to sensitize you all about the danger behind it. Do not be deceived by the sweet words of those who pretend or claim to love you. The truth is that they are not in love but in lust. Their words are sweeter than honey but become bitter at the end. Do you all hear me?" She submitted.

"Yes!!!"

"Do not allow any boy to deceive you into sining against your creator; keep your body holy for your husband, don't allow vain boys to devour your pride and dignity. Once you lose it, you have lost it forever. Boys and girls! Be wise and do not to be ignorant of the devices that are used to deceive young people. I don't want any of my students to drop out of school due to unwanted pregnancies. I want to see you all in the future as great men and women, but becoming great in life depends on the decision you make now. Everyone has his and her own choice to make. Choose the right path. Unity High School!!!"

All shouted: "Unity stands Forever !!!".

She dismissed the assembly. Everyone went to their various classes, forming clusters of side talks.

I was helping mother with her hair when the echo of Mrs. Anthony's words interrupted my thoughts. The words she doled out to the students in the school made me to realize that the love father and mother shared for so long must be strong for them to have got married. I asked mother about her love life father. She expressed her love for him in glowing terms and slowly explained how they met each other. I enjoyed listening to her.

"I knew no man until I met your father", she said it proudly "and I hope you do the same for your husband". If this type of love existed between mother and father how could such misfortune visit our home and tear everything apart? As far as I am concerned, their love cannot fade away because I see that love in mother's eyes every day that passes.

Mother became sad and lonely for those months that her husband was away from the house; she became emaciated as tears became the regular antidote she employed to ease her mind as her days of loneliness increased. She would order Mary to change father's bed sheet every weekend even though father was not around to make use of his room; she does that to keep his presence alive in the house, always checking the phone perhaps father had called.

"No Madam", Mary will say each time mother ordered her to check the phone box for father's call.

We got home tired coming through heavy traffic on the way from Sunday service. The traffic frustrated many drivers as one could tell from their writhed faces. Those who do not have air conditioners in their cars wound down their car window glass to allow some air into the car so as to reduce the heat. I went straight to my room to change while mother prepared a meal of pasta for lunch. She wore one of the blouses father bought for her; I guess this one is a special gift for their wedding anniversary.

"Oyin, when is your exam starting?"

"In a fortnight" I said calmly.

She tilted her head backwards on the chair , using her left hand as a brace. I wanted to ask if she needed anything but I could tell all she wanted was to rest.

"Just a headache that will not allow me to sleep" she said when she saw that I was troubled by her state.

"Should I call the driver so that we can take you to the hospital?"

"Not necessary. I'll be fine." She said, "just a

headache and dizziness, so please don't worry too much my dear."

I was confused as I didn't know what to do to pull her back into form. I know she's indisposed but her insistence on not seeing the med made me helpless. I n addition, her temperature became very high.

"Mary, bring me a bowl of water and a towel."

We had to take her to the hospital when the cold massage didn't work. The doctor ran some tests on her and assured me that she will be fine. It was a restless night for me and the next day I couldn't go to school as I resumed early by her bedside at the hospital. She was surprised to see me so early in the morning without my uniform.

"Are you not going to school today?"

"No! I want to stay by your side." I said with a little smile in my face.

"Your exams?"

"It is next week."

"Study well to be the best my dear."

"I'll do my best." I assured her.

The doctor walked in later for the ward round. "'You're alright now ma'm. We'll discharge you today", he said. "The test carried out shows you are three months pregnant." He submitted.

"Doctor, are you sure? Mother jumped happily to her feet to confirm the words she heard.

"Yes madam", the doctor said proudly with a smile on his face. "Congratulations!", he said again before leaving the ward.

The good news made my stomach feel like it had butterflies in it. There arose a sudden melody in my heart, and tears of joy rolled down my cheeks freely as mother and I embraced one another very tight.

Mother and I nursed the pregnancy as it grew, and all necessary checks and care were duly observed, all at appropriate times.

Few years after mother's last miscarriage, joy filled our home again.

My dream of having a younger one was finally coming to fruition. I thought about father and wished he was present so that we can all welcome this new baby into the family.

Jeff Underwood

Born Jeff Kirk Underwood on December 8th, 1950.

He is a graduate of the University of Washington, Seattle, Washington, where he holds a degree in Psychology. He worked as a Registered Nurse from 1984 to 2007. Here what he has to say about his nursing career: "Writing is my passion. Should have skipped the long nursing career and gone straight to what I truly love".

He is a prolific author with over twenty books to his credits, a number of which he co-authored with Kate Taylor.

"To write and complete a piece is akin to giving birth. Though it is full of pain and challenge, the outcome is worth any difficulty prior."

AN AFRICAN FASCINATION

There was a small lake north of the city of Seattle which was very popular with the people of the area. It was very unique. There was no obvious inflow or outflow of water but the lake's level remained the same and was almost always clean and clear. Once upon a time, there had been an aqua theater there where water shows had been staged for enthusiastic audiences. All that remained of that outdoor extravaganza now was a concrete husk of a quarter-circle of benches and many stairs climbing to its top.

Also, just a short circuit away was a very quaint and still active indoor theater that ran from spring through the very early fall. The plays were light and frothy usually and seated only a small group of individuals at once. It was from there that he and she were exiting.

It was somewhat late evening but was a very balmy one as well. The usual brisk breeze was nearly dormant and only fluffed her hair in an occasional puff or two.

She tickled his palm as they proceeded forward, she got him finally to hold her hand, and she insisted, "A walk around the lake, kind gentleman?" She played obviously coy and batted her beautifully long lashes at him just to emphasize that she would get her way.

And she did. "Love to do that with you, sweet woman."

So they held hands, an Ethiopian woman and a Hispanic man, and even let their connected arms swing back and forth in rhythm to their gait too. Were a stranger to glance at them, that person would never recognize the freshness of it all. Though their unconscious show was full of energy, it didn't seem self-conscious or brand new whatsoever.

They pointed out the lily pads that grew along the shoreline, tried to identify the types of trees that towered over them, pointed at the variety of birds that swooped down on branches, and occasionally laughed at the tiny jumping fish that would arch upward and then plop downward with the tiniest splash.

She was dressed in spring theater gear for Seattle. That would be casual and usually with layers over her shoulders and torso. She had already removed the cognac colored thin leather jacket and he had already taken it and slung it over his shoulder just so she wouldn't have to bother with it. Her blouse was in a white that possessed sheer chiffon insets at the shoulders which gave it a see through look there. Her mocha skin visible through those two portions of the top contrasted beautifully with the rest of the woven item. The long sleeves did give it a slightly more formal look but it worked well for the trek that they were engaged in too. Her plain black toreador pants were just chic enough for the indoor event and just comfortable enough for the outdoor. The only difficult items in her ensemble were her heels. But she made them work for her even when they strolled at a rapid pace.

He was turned on as hell but wasn't about to ogle someone so wonderful this early on in their developing connection. Slow and sensitive and parallel to their mutual emotions was how he was going to take it.

"I have to go back to my African fascination with you. Remember our very first conversation? I have a thing for that continent. And Ethiopia, most ancient land of ancient lands, is the perfect point for us to get to know each other even better.

"I have a game that I will play with you for as long as you will allow it. It is simple. It's called the question game. I am a really curious person. I will ask one question and then when you are done answering, I will ask another."

"Lovely game. Ask away."

"If you could only chose one aspect of Ethiopia to tell me about, something that you know something about, that you love or cherish, regale me with it."

"Regale you with it? You have such an adorably intellectual way of expressing yourself. No one talks like you do. It's something that piques and soothes me all at the same time. Never before and probably never after you."

He hoped that there would never be anyone after him. But that was way jumping the gun!

"There is Lalibela."

"Lalibela?"

"Yes, Lalibela. You asked." And she tightened her grip on his hand and kissed it besides.

"I really feel lighter when I am around you."

They leaned in and kissed quickly. Public displays of affection were no big deals for either of them. The spontaneity of it was incredibly sweet.

"I know this place, this Lalibela, like the back of my hand. When I was living in Ethiopia, I frequented it all the time. Whenever I go back to visit my parents and family there, it is my first stop after Gondar.

"Do you wish the history or the description first?"

"Give me the description first. That way, I can visualize it while you let me in on its origins."

"Description then.

"It is a magnificent set of huge churches hewn right out of the rock of the plateau. It is one of our holiest of cities in Ethiopia. Aksum may be just barely more special spiritually. But Lalibela is a mecca and many pilgrims go there daily."

She was obviously in love with this special area and the significance of it.

Her descriptions were detailed and faultless. She did regale him and here is what she told him.

The layout was that of eleven churches altogether divided into two main groupings. Roughly half of them had been built north of the Jordan River and the remainder to the south. The final church was set aside, a distance away from the ten but was connected by trenches that eased the way there.

The stone was hewn into blocks which were then chiseled further to establish doors, windows, columns, floors, and roofs. On top of that, the hollowing was expanded to include drainage ditches, trenches, and ceremonial passages. She raved about the fact that some of the interconnected walkways had openings to catacombs and caves. She mentioned reverentially that this was a work that brought forth the best blend of mankind and God.

The church, Biete Medhani Alem with its five aisles, was the single largest stone carved monolithic church of its kind. She assured him that its bold design was truly a paean to God Almighty. And it was, in her mind, a testament to man's love of his divine roots made manifest in these wonderful temples devoted to the Christian faith. She continued by mentioning to him that several of the churches were early on used as royal quarters for those of the Zagwe, those of the resurging faith that had waned for a short period. Soon though, they became the temple for just God and his closest minions.

He couldn't believe how much she was aware of this part of her people's legacy.

There in the church of Biet Golgotha replicas of the tomb of Christ, the tomb of Adam, and the crib of the Nativity sat in chiseled glory.

"The churches, because of their popularity, are constantly being restored and returned to their original form."

She revealed to him that there was always some

degradation of the structure and its integrity occurring. Interior paintings, sculptures, and bas relief designs were at the highest of risk. She had donated many Ethiopian birr to the cause of those upgrading and refurbishing projects monotonously going on.

"To give money to this reaches into my heart. It is the very least that I can do."

"Wow!" was all that he uttered.

Not too intellectual, that!

"Ready for the history behind the magnificence now?"

"Totally, totally, totally."

Here she wonderfully articulated to him the pride that she felt in informing him of something quite extraordinary. The cathedrals had been created as a New Jerusalem in the mind of its creator, King Lalibela. After all, the Muslims of King Lalibela's time had conquered the original Holy Lands and had blocked any pilgrimages there by Christians. So, what better an idea than to have established a new area for worship?

And that had been exactly what he did. Or so some of the postulation went according to this wonderful historian at his side.

She explained to him that her sister had gone there once with a man. That was where they had fallen in love. While there, a monk had spoken to them and had pressed upon them the notion that Lalibela as sole, or even likely creator, was suspect.

This sister had passed the story on to her. "You are the recipient of it now."

Scholars, according to this monk, had been in grave disagreement on the origins. The first "facts" mentioned by this venerable old man of the church had been regarding the common legend.

King Lalibela had been born in Roha, Lalibela first, and his name meant, "The bee recognizes its sovereignty."

It had been God who, in a dream, had ordered the

king to build these marvels. In the dream, God had given Lalibela detailed instructions on the construction down to their colors. The construction had moved rapidly as angels had supposedly redoubled the work at night when the laborers of the day had slept.

A second possibility went like this according to the monk. Lalibela had been poisoned by his brother, the treacherous Harbay, and Lalibela had dropped into a three day repose that hadn't been intended as repose whatsoever. In that accidental unconscious state, he had been escorted to heaven and had been given the blueprint of the city to be founded.

Another hypothesis had been that the famous king had been in exile in Jerusalem and had promised himself that when he returned to his native Ethiopia, he had to craft a city to match that of the Holy City.

Finally, there had been rumors that Lalibela had nothing to do with its building and that the Knights Templar from Europe had actually performed the huge task. That, though, as she began to run out of breathe, had been given the least regard of all the myriad fables. Let Africans be the ones to have been the architects of this glory.

They accomplished the entire circuit of the lake while she spoke.

It was time. He couldn't stand it anymore. This woman was priceless and he whispered to her as they slipped into his car, "Come to my place. Pretend it has the grandeur of Lalibela. You can do that by closing your eyes as soon as we go in the door. I will lead you the rest of the way."

She was flushed and exhausted by then. But she had a premonition that there was a perfect antidote for that.

"Lead on. Take me where you desire."

She let all of her secrets out with those two very simple statements.

His heart pounded and the drive swept by without a

conscious effort on his part. His entire mind was focused on the beautiful woman beside him and seeing her safely home to his abode.

She let him pull her hand gently once they were there. She more than appreciated a man who could take her by that very hand and direct her in dominant fashion. His passion was setting an energy within that was sweeping him away. To her, it seemed dominant; to him it seemed wild and crazy. Fortunately, it worked for both.

Now they could have waited and followed some imaginary protocol as to what was appropriate before intimacy's finger lickin' beauty struck.

They weren't so inclined. Even the three buttons on her blouse seemed three too many to them both. She writhed with him then and helped him with her fuchsia bra.

She cupped her plentiful mounds for him and he came to her proffered tips in a swoon as if he were Lalibela set to strike his tool against sacred stone for the first time.

****

As the author, it is actually me, not the characters, who is fascinated with Africa. It is the land of mankind's birth and I especially fell in love with the cathedrals and churches hewn out of rock faces in Lalibella, Ethiopia. I am enchanted by the various origin stories of that wonderful architecture too. There was a suggestion in my research that this was not created at the hand of African's. I call that nonsense. Africans are masterful and resourceful, then and now. Africans built this monument and testament to the heavens and I am proud to understand that

Kate Taylor

She hails from a tiny town, Jaffrey, New Hampshire, in the northeastern part of the United States. She is the author of The Pink Eraser, and many books with co-author, Jeffrey Underwood.

Her most recent work is Captive to Cocoa, an eye opener to child trafficking and labour in many parts of the world.

"Call me Kate. I like that. I am a writer! I am an author! I am a poet! I provide opportunities for meaningful activities for the elderly. I love steaming hot coffee, juicy pears and jasmine bubble baths! I am from New Hampshire, which makes it all, 'wicked' good!".

Jeff and Kate blog via http://long-distance-writing.blogspot.com/

OPAL'S DREAM

It had been some time since Opal had been victim to one of her nightmares.

She *was* stronger now and wondered how she would react, should the horrific visitors come to attack her mind at night again. She tried to put the idea of the nightmares out of her head. She talked to herself before going to sleep and thought about her writing, cheerful picnics, and most of all, getting into her little wabi sabi red truck, fitting herself into the driver's seat and turning the key. There would be a very special person as passenger. She could see herself with the windows rolled down and her red hair blowing in the breeze, wearing her pink shirt and her favorite overalls. Driving towards the pink and turquoise sunset. "Pink skies at night, sailor's delight"…Knowing that at this moment, life would start anew.

She sighed every time she thought of this vision. It could come true, couldn't it? Why did she question herself? She was able to identify her feelings now and was able to process them and speak their truth. Opal was well on her way to being healthy and enjoying healthy relationships.
However, even the most pleasant of thoughts would give way and a dark place in her mind that resisted going away would take over. Always a reminder that Opal needed to remain vigilant in her healing, one day at a time, and if need be, one hour at a time, even one more nightmare at a time.

For no reason, this Sunday afternoon nap was restless

and fitful. An hour this time, into calm sleep, when her brain would try to make the changeover from the first level to the next, the dream would come to her once again. The clock was ticking its tick, tick, tick, the spider tiptoed across the floor and under the bureau, and even in the daytime, the nightlight glowed and a soft fragrance emanated from the bowl on top to lull her to sleep. Opal tossed and turned, quilt on, quilt off; her mind knew exactly what was coming.

Yes! Again! Oh, please.... Not today!

This time, she heard the yelling and screaming first. Someone was out to get her. Opal heard the noise, the threats and knew that she had to run! She screamed inside her own mind, "Hurry! Don't think! Just run!"

Where was the noise coming from?! Who was it that was going to kill her now?! There was no time to think! Opal had to run and so she did. Breathlessly. Stumbling but staying upright, running as fast as she could.

She looked around! The weather was sunny. It was day time. If it was day time, others must have seen this! Why wouldn't they come to help?! Opal kept running, hearing the screams from behind!

"I will get you this time! You are not getting away from me!" "Do you hear me?!" "Come back!" "STOP NOW!"

But, Opal didn't stop. She kept running and running. Down the sidewalk where the concrete had cracked. Oh, she might slip! Now, onto the road, the tar, aged but smoother, she was safer running on this surface.

"I said Stop!" "When I get my hands on you, I will kill you!!"

The voice seemed to be catching up! Opal ran faster still! There's had to be a place to hide where she would be safe and hidden from this perpetrator, this would be murderer, but where?! Into the school yard! Surely, there would be people there to help!

Agh! There was no one! Fences! Opal felt pain in her

chest; tightening, clenching pain! The searing pain constricted her airway!

"Stop right there! You are going to be dead soon, missy!!" Again the voice shouted, "When I get my hands on you, I will use them to kill you!"

Omigod! The voice was right behind her! Opal saw a red truck and made a dash to jump onto the back. There was a bright blue plastic tarp in the truck and Opal crawled underneath to hide. Her heart was pounding out of her chest. Her breathing was loud and rapid, she tried to settle it, so as not to be heard.

She heard the footsteps seeming to run past, and then they stopped. It was quiet. Excruciatingly quiet. Dead silence. Maybe just maybe they were gone. It was then that Opal felt a hand grab her leg and begin to pull her from the back of the truck!

"I've got you now. You are dead!!" This was when Opal usually awakened with a near silent scream, one that bolted her from the bed in a sweat. Never seeing who wanted to hurt her. But… this time was different. She turned around and…Omigod!! What the..?!

This time, Opal did not awaken. Opal was ready for a fight! The person who had been trying to get her, the monster, the alien, the chaser, all along...

It was Opal!!!

She was the one, but she was not the beautiful, soft, pink, loving, and caring Opal. No!

This Opal was hideous, zombie looking, hair dirty and sticking up everywhere, filthy white tee shirt, ripped and torn jeans, and no shoes. Her face distorted, as if she had come back from the dead. This horrific Opal had garish makeup, her lipstick drawn on misshapen lips that stretched to her ears. It was the sick, bad, evil part of herself.

Opal kicked the hideous self away with all her might. She moved further back in the red truck, while she searched her overalls pocket for the tiniest bit of what was left of the pink eraser. There was neither notebook nor pencil now how would she do this?! Think fast!

Her evil self was climbing into the truck now, holding her hands up, ready to grasp Opal by the neck, ready to kill her!

NO!!!!!

Opal held up the pink eraser and moved it in front of the evil Opal, as if she were erasing her face, between her eyes, over her nose and down through the center of her. Opal worked rapidly rubbing and rubbing, moving herself in fear, further backwards in the bed of the truck.

Slowly, as if a costume was loosening its skin tight grip, the shell of the evil Opal began to slip off the sides of the face. Like a snake shedding its skin, it was gathering like cloth and wrinkling as it began falling away from her body.

What was coming through the tiniest ray at a time was a pearlescent ivory glow, and a new Opal revealed.

The new Opal was radiant with all her soft pink skin showing, wispy and almost transparent, as if a spirit. It *was* her spirit, herself that had been hidden under pain and fear for so very long.

The pink spirit Opal embraced her in the back of the truck. The embrace was warm and Opal sensed the aroma of a soft floral fragrance.

Little by little, spirit Opal entered into her solid self, and Opal felt the glow of her spirit within her.

She was calm and lulled back to sleep by the floral fragrance. She slumbered peacefully.

When she awoke, she was in the back of the red truck. She was not sure that she was fully awake, yet. Looking around, feeling late day sunshine on her, Opal knew she had to be awake. She remembered the dream. She felt warm inside; her spirit was almost palpable. She still smelled the soft aroma of flowers. What was real? Was it all real?

Opal got out of the truck and walked around it. Oh

my! It was the wabi sabi red truck she had dreamed about. On the side of the truck, she saw what was written in shabby script the words "Betty Jane." And in the back, the license plate "LIPSTIK".

Keys were in the ignition.

Opal got inside the truck, looked it all over. It wasn't new at all, and that is why she loved it. The tiny piece of pink eraser, blackened on the edges and only as big as her fingernail, showed very little pink. She opened the glove box and tucked the pink eraser inside.

She started the truck and looked up. There he was. Standing by the side of the road, smiling, with two thumbs up. She drove close to him and motioned for him to get in. They touched hands and shared the softest of kisses.

She smiled and whispered, afraid she might wake herself up, "Let's go," and they began the drive into the swirls of pink and turquoise sunset.

Her red hair blowing out the open window, all comfortable in her pink shirt and overalls. With a special passenger beside her.

This was not a dream.

****

This short story was taken from the book, The Pink Eraser by me, Kate Taylor.

Opal and I share the same story.

The nightmares were real. The fright was real. Over fifty years of pain. The book was written about my life in a time of great healing. The process of healing was difficult and a lot of hard work.

The nightmares ended. They have returned no more. The healing is a work in progress.

Higher Power watches over me and is my true and loving support.

Running in fear over a lifetime does not heal. Turning to and acknowledging the pain and its thoughts can be the first steps in the process of becoming healthy

'Lakunle Jaiyesimi

He is a Pharmacist cum lecturer at the Obafemi Awolowo University, Ile-Ife, Nigeria and a writer. He blogs at http://lakunlescrews.wordpress.com and http://ifepoetryportal.wordpress.com. He has written and managed the production of several plays, one of which is *Akanni-Opomulero*. To his credit are several short stories and poems like *Rest in Jail*, *The Sepulcher*, *Death* and *Naked Flower*. He produces story-telling sessions for children, *Alo Iya Agba* and poses as an Idea Consultant.

A DANCE OF SHAME

As he paced onto the airplane, he was only emphatically aware of the well-groomed three-piece suit he had on, with the matching Ferrari hat that stood out tall even in the night. His disguise was almost a loud statement as Ibrahim took his final steps on the soil of Nigeria.

The last three years, since Ibrahim converted to the other religion, has offered a harrowing experience for him with the members of the dreaded sect, Harom Kobom being perpetually on his trail; as commandeered by top guns.

On three occasions, according to personal account, he has received direct threats from a particular man, who always signed his name, Anonymous. On one of such unsettling occasions, Ibrahim was seated in a front pew while the priest , decked in his flowing cassock, ministered to individuals . An unsealed note was passed to him by a hand just next to him absentmindedly, like it was some open-secret business pamphlet. On absorbing the contents of the note, his palms gathered sweat as he could also feel either his body or the seat upon which he sat vibrating against the other. He managed to raise his head to inspect who it was that handed him the note.

The heavy build and beard-filled face of the man made him quite uneasy; the sermonizing voice of the priest was shut out against his ears and the hitherto haphazard movements around him ceased for that moment. He only cared about the man next to him. Even though he was motionless, he was making a progressive advance towards Ibrahim as far as he was concerned. He imagined the man bringing out a piece of sharp knife, stabbing him in the right ear and screwing it further in. He imagined the worst and he could not bear the thoughts any longer.

Abruptly, he got up and made to run but a hand dragged him back to his seat. Helpless, lost and sweaty, he sat till the end of the priest's rituals and quietly awaited his fate. He was dead, lost to himself; he could not scream as he imagined that would be cut short by the cold feel of a piercing knife in his ear.

Time passed, he heard the conciliatory tick-tocks of the clock but it was not; it was the sound of the approaching steps of the priest. Ibrahim was startled by the cold feel of the hands of the priest over his ears. He yelled as he sprang up but he was again held back by the hand that earlier dragged him back to his seat. It was the arm of the chair he sat on that pinned the hem of his dress. He wrestled it free and would not wait to consider the words of the priest. In a moment, he was beyond the door sprinting away as fast as his feet could carry him. The priest watched till he disappeared.

At a distance, in a safe haven away from the eyes of those who haunted him, Ibrahim reclined against a wall, brought out the piece of paper earlier handed to him and read the contents again.

"Dear Ex, I rejoice with you on your conversion from our fold, the home of your brothers, to the other...but I regret to say you have few nights more to remain alive. Against our advice to you to live and let live; and not to kill in order not to get killed, you still went to the press to kill your brothers, though ex, in public. Therefore, for running your mouth and mentioning names, the little sacrifice is just one life...yours!"

In the dead of the night, Ibrahim crept out of the haven and sought out the priest, who had earlier promised to make arrangements to fly him out to meet his long-lost-but-recently-found sister in faraway Norway. He had earlier rejected the offer of the trust of his new God and distrust of man, both priest and sister. But in the security of life, no other considerations are made; run or hide, whichever is suitably relevant. So he did, helped by the priest, he found himself on the airplane comfortably seated in his outstanding dress.

Midair, after having had a serving of coffee, Ibrahim adjusted himself to ensure he had a lively trip. He had a thought on his mind with which he intended to start up a conversation with whoever sat beside him, 'National security concerns'. Ibrahim looked to his side and the first word he successfully framed in his mouth got stuck when he saw the man seated beside him. It was the same heavy-build, beards-filled-faced man that sat beside him on the pew.

He recognized him instantly and the horrid feeling he had associated with the man came back to him without his consent. Effortlessly, he brought out a pen and a sheet of paper and began to scribble a lengthy collection of words. At the end of the exercise, he inspected what he has written; satisfied, he folded it up and replaced it in his upper pocket, got up and walked briskly to the rear of the plane. He was out of sight.

Fifteen minutes more in the air and the plane was land-bound. The landing jolted a number of people awake, including the beard-filled-faced man. It did not seem that anyone noticed his protracted absence, as all on board got off board with no concern for his whereabouts.

However, there was a woman impatiently waiting with a cardboard bearing 'IBRAHIM'. She was in an argument with the crew of the airline; standing just beside her, a little aloof, was the beard-filled-faced man, who slept most of the journey and was, like every other passenger, unable to account for Ibrahim's whereabouts.

In the heat of it all, a hostess came along and delivered a note she had picked up in the toilet and which bore a phrase, "Dear sister...From Ibrahim...". The so-called sister retrieved the letter, browbeat, and gave stern instructions, while facing the direction of the bearded man, that Ibrahim be sought out and apprehended at all costs. Such could be said to be unbecoming of a sister.

'Dear sister' retreated to have a private time with Ibrahim's note. "Dear sister, take these as the last words of a dead me to you. It is sad enough that it has to come to this. I regret that I finally gathered the strength, well out of no choice, to say goodbye to you. What I regret the more is the fact that my goodbye has to come without seeing you in spite of all my efforts and sacrifices ;at least this one time.

Everything is clearer to me now. Dad, mum, you and I crashed with Dad's bike on our way back home that fateful day. I was only two at the time and the accident was fatal. I lost three of you in the accident; but I was later told that a good priest had taken pains to transfer your bodies to the morgue. In good condition, except the need for a few stitches here and there. I was picked by a sheikh-to-be, who took me to his home full of women and children, personally stitched my wounds and… Well, what better kind of life would I have lived if not that of an early independence with no self-support system; the type of autonomy an irresponsible federal government would be willing to give her federating states.

I joined the almajiris on the streets and that was a defining moment for me; it marked the last time I would think about family. I saw myself in the middle of the world, alone; caring for myself however well or not I could manage it, with no thought whatsoever to whomever has his or her ox gored in the process. I did whatever I wanted and went wherever I liked. Where would I sleep daily if not wherever the earth permitted me on her face?
It was a scorched life! A life of begging and wishing death to those who refused to give. The pang of hunger is incomparable to being homeless or to growing under the watchful eyes of the sun or being bathed perpetually by the rain and the storms.

Some men who came by were generous and others were not; while some would pay for food sufficient to go round the majority of us, some delighted in watching us as we fought over their remnants, injuring ourselves with all kinds of objects in the process. Fondly, but regretfully, I remember one of such men that we once ambushed. This was a man, who had made it his daily leisure to leave very little food in his plate for almost a hundred of us. He was sure we would run for it like ants. And true-to-type, we did. He would usually sit in a corner, one leg over the other, beside the woman who sold him food. They would laugh, laugh and laugh at our folly. I hated the sight of them; even now that I regret our actions, I resent them.

As seasons passed, we planned and one day, we did carry out our plans. We impatiently waited around for him on his way to the restaurant. After hours of waiting, he got to the middle of where we were planted, and we went for him. What we did to him that day was so brutal that no one ever saw him in the restaurant again; not even in that vicinity. I would not know if he died afterwards, but I would expect it.

Dear sister, that event marked for me the beginning of a blind-eyed wicked life. I continued that life, growing up on the streets, ignored by both the constituted government and the informal government (people, ordinary men, who go by daily).

My friends and I all did unthinkable things; in order to survive a system that only thrived on what you get for yourselves, as exemplified by those who should care for others but would not. We did things that can only be imagined than heard. I would hate to recount them myself; the details are gory, and these went on and on for several years into our adulthood. The country seemed to look the other way until a group of 'benevolent' brothers came to draw us in. They helped us properly harness our strengths, abilities and humanities (or inhumanities, in retrospect) as a group against an identified enemy, which was what we have always done albeit unorganized.

Thanks to Harom Kobom that gave us another lease of life, at least, so I thought. And wherever you are in the world, be it Norway, New York, Addis Ababa, Moscow, Abuja, even in the deep of the earth, the acts perpetrated by us cannot be strange to your ears. It's always been in the news. But I wish to assure you sister, in spite of what I believe now and whatever it is they say in the news, or peddle about us, we were victims of an improperly led society, as much as our victims were too. Everyone is unsafe! If they did not die in our bomb explosions, we would have died to hunger, neglect and the scorching sun. Those victims were as innocent as we were. The only criminals were their leaders as well as ours. They all used us as pawns.

I realized these and chose to pull out of the group. You can be assured, pulling out was not as easy as deciding to. But pull out I did and through a process was able to become a new creature as they always say.

My troubles with the man, Anonymous, did not start until a moment of flippancy when I granted a radio reporter an interview session. There, amongst other things, I mentioned that I was a member of the Harom Kobom group and told the curious reporter about some of the many operations I was involved in. Since then, Anonymous has been on my trail.

On the day that I attended my first open-air crusade organized by the priest, I was shocked by his revelations, as he painstakingly told the story of my family. He mentioned how he took you, dad and mum to the morgue and just before the final rituals on your corpse, he noticed your left eye twitched. He held up the rituals much longer, during which time you came around. It was a testimony of God's wonders as far as he was concerned, but at the time I was hearing it, it was with mixed feelings. My sister was alive; he even mentioned that he had been in contact with her ever since. How could it be?

I could not wait for the crusade to end; I walked up to the priest and had a long conversation with him. I remorsefully told him about my past and the present, where a Mr. Anonymous was after my life. Fatherly, he assured me all will be well and promised to assist me as much as he could. He would fly me out of the sight of Anonymous or any other prying eyes, for good, to the waiting arms of my sister, wherever you were.

It sounded too good to be true, and for many other reasons, I rejected the offer until the day I sat in a pew beside one bearded man. That was the day after the second time I would grant a reporter an interview session. This time, the talk was lengthier as I had much to say. I needed leverage; I needed to place a value on my life even if death would come unannounced. So, I deliberately went to demand for the session, where I mentioned names of colleagues and our top sponsor.

That was it; they got angry and would not have more of me! Sister, I have since been trailed practically everywhere, tracked, ambushed and spied on. This is what informed this trip of mine; an escape from my shadow. However, my shadow is as obstinate as all shadows. On a trip to the arms of my sister wherever she was; a trip I believe only the priest and I know about, seated right beside me is a man, whose sudden appearance wherever I was had never been without the attendant fear of losing my life in an instant.

Or could I be wrong? Sister, am I hallucinating? Is there likelihood that all atrocities I've committed are haunting me? Well, I doubt; I still recognize my face in the mirror.

Dear sister, I have a short time. Here I am on my way to a sister, I have never met or known, on the instructions of a priest I have started not to trust; sitting beside a bearded man I have come to be scared of. Could he be Anonymous?

I've made my decision and I'm gone; gone forever. It

is better I take my life 'in' my hands than for someone to take it for me.

I have been a victim of a derailed society; I have made many more victims of that society. Many are currently walking the streets as victims and victims to be. How many more would we have? Sister, I need your reaction, how many more before we say, ENOUGH.

A DIRGE FOR HOPE

A well-groomed lawn beautified the terrace outside an old building that was used as a makeshift church for Living Hope for the Nations. The Church was founded by a friend of mine with whom I attended University. It was a church that prided herself in giving hope to the hopeless; an act one may need the lens to be able to observe. Akinokun Fatomilola (Now Daniel Jesutomilola) always had a feminine touch to his sermons, generating all manners of noise from time to time. He had not changed. With the final words fading off the megaphones that were stationed outside the old building came the pouring out of humans who faithfully attended the church. They seemed upbeat as they descended on the only rough-edged stone that sat at the bottom of the entrance into the church, going their separate ways. Some waited nearby to chat and laugh and exchange warm pleasantries.

I watched as I sat patiently in my newly-bought second-hand Toyota Camry, ninety nine model. I did not tell my friend I'd visit him; I planned to surprise him. It's been seven years since we graduated and haven't crossed paths, but I got news of his present location and business from a mutual friend. I was not so much taken aback by the news that he finally ended up a Pastor but, without showing any sign of it, I was shocked that my friend, in spite of his gospel mission, kept up his fondness for sticks of cigarette and bottles of wine. Not that religion expressly forbids it, it was just a 'simple and harmless likeness', he would counter my objections.

The few church members, who hung around and who were privileged to behold the surprise of their Pastor Daniel Jesutomilola on seeing me, with his juvenile conviviality when he finally met up with me; along with his child less wife, would not believe that our next stop as we both left the church premises shortly after was a palm-wine joint. But there we were, reliving old memories in person.

Mama Ekene, who sold us palm-wine as students, had passed on and Ekene had become the father of the house. He had a wife, who assisted in attending to customers and a kid, who played with the dirty water held in a big bathing bowl at a corner, with all the liberty anyone could pray for in the world.

Pastor Daniel would have none of my objections to his drinking palm-wine and smoking a few sticks on occasions, as he waved such aside. Well, I thought, this was not as worse as what you find elsewhere, especially in far-away Lagos where I lived. Ile-Ife was a beautiful town! So, I followed his lead as we drank, sweated and told stories of events in-between us and the years gone by.

None of all the stories he shared with me, not even his wife's barrenness and its unfortunate cause, or the strange death of some of his church members, or his recent inclusion in a clandestine political team saddled with the responsibility of creating some laws guiding the conduct of the grassroots people, fascinated me as much as his disdainful mention of a group of four boys, who particularly menaced his church members as they went to and left church every Sunday.

He didn't know their names. That was good because if he had, it must have been in accounts recorded with the police after having had them arrested. He said he always thought of getting them arrested but never mustered enough courage to carry it out. The boys only gathered in front of the church on service days, be it weekdays or Sundays; but Sundays seemed to be their favorite because of the large population of people who attended service on that sunny day.

The four boys were one of the hundreds of

thousands of other unemployed youth, who lurk around in public or in their parents' houses, doing nothing. In order not to remain hopelessly pathetic, they chose to be useful to themselves and the community by applying themselves and in the process making a decent living. Strategically, they had discovered that the church provided all they needed.

In addition to the large population of her members, the church was located just where the road was in a bad state; and the name of the church was attractive enough "Living Hope for the Nations". The boys would position themselves at the bad portion of the road, filling up the gaping gorges with sand that they collected elsewhere. They exaggerated all their efforts in order to be noticed easily by those who drove along the road; at least, they were certain the church members of Living Hope would not miss them.

On a bright day when the god of luck was indeed happy, the four boys would go home with between five hundred and one thousand naira to share amongst themselves. A large chunk of such money was obtained from road users other than my friend's church members as he proudly informed me that he continuously discouraged them from giving money to 'those area boys, who may turn around to become armed robbers'. He hinted the possibility of the boys being the robbers who have robbed and terrorized the town continuously in recent times. No other person thinks so, but Pastor Daniel has always maintained that stance and has told whoever cared to listen.

I objected, and in spite of the support I received from some other palm-wine drinkers who sprawled everywhere under Ekene's thatched bar, my friend would not admit that those boys were likely, no; most likely, not the robbers that terrorized the town; and that they were contrarily doing more good than harm to the town. The rate of accidents had reduced drastically since they started filling up the gorges. By the virtue of their chosen work, they have reduced the probability of unemployed youth becoming robbers and are serving as role models to others. Although, one should wonder why the gorges they filled never ever got filled up; there was that possibility that they went back every night to excavate whatever earth they had filled in during the day, just to ensure they had work to do the following day. It was better than robbery but my friend and the members of his Living Hope for the Nation church looked the other way. Perpetually!

In no time, we were short of stories to tell having been slightly intoxicated. Ekene's wife was at the time clearing the shop and putting in place the kegs, emptied bottles and turned-over calabashes. Ekene, who sat close by and visibly intoxicated himself, looked calm as he awaited his wife's summon to lock up and go home. Our fellow drinkers were leaving one after another, leaving a few of us behind. I tapped Pastor Daniel to down the remaining contents of his calabash so as to head home. I thought to myself that his wife must be aware of his daily indulgence in wine. Staggering but recovering normal gaits, we left the shop and parted ways.

I survived drunk -driving that night and I am aware Pastor Daniel did too. His sermonizing sessions were broadcast on cable television every Sunday of the last few months. He always appeared prim like a man that had never been overcome by the powers of wine. Almost immaculate! That night and through many nights after, I kept thinking about the four boys who my friend touted as a menace to his church, but who earned a honest living by making the government-abandoned road passable in their own way. What better way to serve humanity! I had thought that the character that menaced the people was Pastor Daniel himself, who extorted hard-earned money from his church members; people that were already mentally, physically and, let's say spiritually, impoverished by all concerned. So sad.

I would have continued to wallow in the thought of many other Nigerian victims of neglect, who were further victimized in the hands of fellow victimized Nigerians capable of it through dubious means like my friend but for the news that came to me in a text message composed by Pastor Daniel, "One of those four boys is dead. He was crushed by a high-speeding truck this morning while service was on. The others fled immediately leaving the body of their man behind. I'm almost certain they will not return. We thank the Lord that now, my church members can come to church and leave anytime without being harassed by layabouts anymore. Praise the Lord!"

THE STORY OF A SINGLE LIFE

Natisha Rinks realized a little too late that she had aged one busy morning when she woke up and could not lift herself out of bed as easily as she had always done. It was a heavy body, especially her legs. She experienced pains that made her cry; pains that would only later be ascribed to arthritis. Then, worry set in and it would only get worse.

As against her personality, Natisha Rinks worried much about her past; she was troubled about her hopes and aspirations. A younger Natisha would have thought life would never cease for her. In all of her plans, there was no place for death.

In the span of thirty five years she had lived as an adult, she lived with seven husbands bearing two kids only for the second. One was now 31 years old and the other, 30. Sasha and Felipe Rinks live far away and apart in busier climes than Lagos and Natisha knew not these places.

Natisha's last marriage ended on a good note for her. She had no plans to remarry but to enter a world of freelancing with any man that suits her; however, she wanted it without any man breathing down her neck. She planned also to voluntarily retire from her job into private consulting, which would free much of her day to allow a romance with her other plans for a good life. She was a good dreamer. She hoped far beyond her arthritic state, where all will be fine again and she would continue her life as she planned.

Alas, here she was, bedridden; halted by a sardonic stroke that took no cognizance of her aspirations. It imposed restrictions on her as a new way of life. On her way back from the last-visited hospital, in company of a driver and well-meaning neighbors , and in spite of the noise and business of road-users, people with a vitality to pursue their aspirations, armed with a hopeless report, Natisha Rinks sat quietly and unaware of her environment like a vegetable off its roots.

Three months after her return from a traditional healer, who had been recommended by a doctor with native intelligence and connection, Natisha Rinks was able to coordinate her movements, though poorly but better than she could before her visit to the hospital. Time would later make this poor movement of hers the norm as she quickly got used to it.

What further kept her alive and her mind vibrant was the noise, with playful attractions, of her three grandchildren, two boys and a girl, whose parents saw relief in their mother's present condition, where nature had conferred on her a nanny status, allowing the parents, Sasha and Felipe Rinks to focus on their busy lives.

In the morning of one of those harrowing, stroke-blemished days in her life, incidentally a public holiday for the grand kids, Natisha Rinks woke up and dragged herself to her spacious and colour-infested sitting room to meet the kids playing rough. The eldest, David Rinks, rammed into his grandmother as soon as she appeared. She staggered but managed to sustain a strong grip on the door frame. Within a fraction of a second and just before she fully realized she was still standing, Cecelia, the girl and the youngest of the three, jumped off a table and at Natisha, though playfully intended. They both crashed with a thud. Natisha expertly pretended she was in no pain and gently sat herself up. With smiles, Natisha Rinks watched the kids as they turned the house into a nightmare she would have hitherto paid any amount to ward off. But now, she smiled at the whole situation, either due to her helplessness or her acceptance that nothing ephemeral, but joy and an inner peace, is worth fighting for.

On the smiling faces and in the bright eyes of her grand kids, Natisha Rinks saw what she had missed or neglected for most of her life – the joy of innocence and the simplicity of the best part of happiness. Seated on the floor, at an almost unnoticeable corner, Natisha appeared like an innocent kid being taught the lessons of life by learned adults, who in this case happen to be her grandchildren.

Natisha sank in the lessons: to achieve happiness, you don't have to step out of your house, getting out of your way. By remaining with a humble approach to life, making the best of your immediate environment and circle of friends and family members, your smile can be genuinely full. By dreaming and over-dreaming and stepping into the worlds of rain and sunshine to achieve your dreams, not bad in themselves, can be the source of many worries, frustration and an ultimate hollow life of sorrows. Again and again, the euphoria of the kids brought gentle smiles to the face of Natisha Rinks.

On Christmas Eve, Sasha and Felipe Rinks arrived from their busy lives along with their wives. They all, without the exception of the little kids, got busy preparing for the larger family reunion scheduled for the next day. Fagged out, everyone retired late, heaving their bodies lazily to bed. Natisha Rinks was the last to sleep; the dying eve was the simplest and the happiest day in her life, she wanted it to linger.

She inspected everyone, tucked in the sheets properly and exposed body parts covered up, before finally retiring to sleep. The night was long for all, but eternal for Natisha Rinks. It brought with it the lasting fulfillment of all her dreams, past and present, uniting them into a concrete resolution of all worries, bliss.

The following day, everyone woke up terribly late but Natisha slept on, caring less for the reunion. She had all she wanted. Having being sated by the fulfillment of her dreams in sleep, Natisha was unaffected by the need to rise to meet the day's routine.

Her family members all came up with a plan to gather at her door and wake her into the new day of reunion and Christmas with songs and merriment. However, their noise refused to disturb her slumber as they found out that her eternal night had become eternity. The family reunion, scheduled to be a gathering for laughter, playful taunts and much eating and drinking, turned into the coming together of mourners.

She passed away quietly and while her sleeping dreams remained fulfilled, her waking dreams remain alive waiting for who will be prepared to take them on and go through the hassles of attempting to achieve them.

Mikail Bashir

Mikail Oluwadare Bashir was born in Kaduna State, Nigeria. He always wanted to be a lawyer from his childhood, but fate drifted him into studying Accounting.

In 1998, he founded Alphabash Musical and Theatre Arts Group; a non-profit entertainment outfit geared towards impacting the society through value-driven projects that tend to correct societal vices via poetry, music, drama and comedy among other things.

His passion for the screen motivated him to study screenwriting in Hampton Court Studio UK, where he obtained a Diploma in Screenwriting (Master class) in 2009. He has been involved in numerous content development projects with Motherwell Integrated System ever since.

He has numerous unpublished playlets, essays, screenplays, short stories and memoires.

At the moment he resides in the United States with his wonderful wife and lovely children. He intends to study MFA in Creative writing some day.

ODE IN WAITING

It was a hot summer afternoon. I woke up to what seemed to be a brief and harmless nap to the poking edges of all sorts of kitchen utensils – spoons, forks and jerk-knife. From nowhere forceful breeze breathed putrid stench into my nostrils and that aroused a feeling of nausea. It reminded me of the day I stepped into an all-cowry decorated calabash full of slimy oblation at a T-Junction, when some disrespectful giant lousy rodents chased after each other and got me startled. The awful image and stench from that offering plagued my imagination for long.

From what seemed a blurred vision in my bleary eyes, I could see the vague figures of people around, most of whom I could not attach any identity to. But their activities were as clear see-through of a crystal ball property. On one side was a woman squeezing layers of onions into my eyes. Another woman tried to force spoon between my dentition; an attempt to achieve what -- I could not fathom. Yet another woman, whom I recognized broke through the throng with a plate containing slimy mixture. It was a mixture of milk and egg yolk beaten together to form yellow ochre. As she mixed the concoction, its smell hit my nose and I nearly threw up. It was then it occurred to me where the breeze got the unsolicited foul message it sent to my nostrils earlier.

'What happened?' I shoved the woman attempting to choke me with the spoon aside until she collided with another onlooker.

'Where is mama?' I asked.

'Alleluia!' a woman chorused from somewhere in the crowd as if the survival of the universe depended on that utterance. By now the crowd grew larger and larger and in a split second I heard an incoherent startling outcry from behind the crowd. The crowd's attention shifted. I recognized that voice. It was a shrill voice that could pierce through a fabric and shred it into tidbits. For me it was only one voice that could conveniently fit in to that space - mama's. Such was the distinctive feature of mama's voice especially when she was edgy or scolding any of us for wrongdoing. But this day, she was not scolding anyone, edgy? Over what? My heart skipped multiple times as I awaited response.

'What's wrong?' It was to no one in particular.

Soon the crowd fizzled out in the middle allowing me to have a glimpse of the object of its spectacle. I saw mama knelt before a fast-approaching car in the middle of the road, her hands clasped in her chest like an errant servant pleading for mercy before his master. She was barely naked with her bedraggled maxi swaying to the tune of the wind. While her wrapper trailed behind her, her scarf ran an errand for whirling wind. The horrid look on her face coupled with the tears that gushed out of her eyes down her jagged face, spoke volume. She would pass for a mentally retarded person. I had never seen her in such deplorable state, at least not in the entire length of my life so far. I was fourteen.

As the car screeched to a halt, people especially those who were oblivious of what prompted her temporal madness, hurled all sorts of unprintable insults at her.
'What is your problem? Are you crazy?!', a passerby exclaimed.

'What is the matter with you?', her companion was enraged, hissing as they passed by.

'What is the matter with you?' a hoarse voice filled the air.

It was the driver's. He had swiftly flung the car door open, and alighted from the car looking down at mama as she tendered her hands pleadingly, pointing towards the direction where I was seated totally drenched. Her words were incoherent. Whatever they were won the empathy of the irked driver as his anger ebbed away and an expression of emotion took over.

It was at this point that I struggled to get up but my attempts were stonewalled by the people around.

'What's wrong with mama?' this time it was to one of the two women who flanked me as *support* amid the medley that ensued. It was an annoying grave silence that greeted me in response. I became tensed.

'Let's carry him to the car.' A woman intoned.

I feel strong. Why are they contemplating carrying me to a car? I wondered.

At this time, a white station wagon car pulled over in front of our backyard where the entire episode of the day unfurled. It was the car that nearly got mama killed. The car door swiftly swung open as mama ran towards me barefooted. She feigned a smile that lasted a few milliseconds as her eyes met with mine.

'Pele.' You will be fine. My Father has never disappointed me…', she said pointing her index finger heavenwards as if she had a vivid glance of whom she was referring to. This had been her pattern of approach to her Maker whenever she was in dire need. '…He will not forsake me this time', she said as she held me tight to her chest placing her arms all around me. I saw a tear escape from her eyes even though she fought hard to hide it. It was about then that a glimpse dawned on me of what had transpired in the episode of that day's chapter. To me what seemed like a simple, harmless nap was unknown to me a gateway to the beyond. I later got to know.

We soon arrived at a nearby private hospital, where I was admitted that evening. Uncle JJJ, who had rushed to the hospital after my younger sister conveyed the message to him of my failing health, was to stay with me, while mama went home to get the things we needed for the duration of the admission. But this was not without her usual protests.

'You go home and take care of his younger ones. I'll sleep and watch over him.' Uncle JJJ offered.

'No, I'll wait', mama protested.

'You need to go home and change into something nice, auntie. Look how tattered you are looking.' He said as his eyes probed her from tip to toe.

Mama scrutinized her dressing, 'I am not looking for a suitor, am I?' They burst into laughter. She gently looked into my eyes, using the back of her palm to feel my temperature.

'He'll be fine. There is nothing to worry about.' Uncle JJJ assured and before she could utter another protest he calmly used a betrayal tactic –

'Or do you want her to stay?' he asked. I smiled as I shook my head in disapproval. Mama shrugged and placed her hands on my forehead and uttered a silent prayer, then left.

The hospital was a modern building painted in titanium white. At the entrance were some array of well trimmed ebullient flowers leading to the porch. Heading towards the OPD, visitors and patients alike were greeted by the zephyr of arranged trees that stood adjacent to one another. At night, the lights flushed on the walls and gave them a perfect wash. As if that wasn't enough, it was a halcyon environment devoid of the usual characteristics of urban cities.

That evening, I laid silently, listening to the smooth blend of sonorous tunes from the canaries that hovered about the nestled trees outside the yard. My head pounded. I began to reminisce on the events that played out earlier that day.
****

I remember I was running a high temperature and couldn't make it to school that morning. All symptoms pointed to malaria, so it was needless going to see the doctor, although seeing the doctor was my last resort irrespective of whatever nature of sickness it may be. The mere thought of syringe gave me jitters and the smell of drugs and all sorts of disinfectants made me sick. So, I took to self medication. It was a couple of malaria drugs. Shortly after I took the drugs, it gagged me and I spurted all about the bed and the floor – yellowish, slimy and smelly.

'What happened?', mama came in just in time. It was a question that never got answered as all attempts to respond provoked the nausea.

I was shivering, with goose bumps all over my body.

'Have you taken the drugs?', I nodded. She felt my temperature from behind her right palm; raised my upper eyelid and looked through and shrugged – a gesture that suggested my temperature was normal. She went into the bedroom and returned almost immediately.

'Take this and wrap it around yourself', it was one of her wrappers – one of the few she wore only on special occasions. I took it and buried myself in it. She adjusted the pillow and promised to return.

I slept off.

By the time I woke up that afternoon, I was relieved of the symptoms. I felt strong. On the table was the evidence of mama's fulfillment of her promise to return. She had wrapped it in a towel to keep it warm. I uncovered the plate and savoured the sumptuous meal. It was plateful of rice and beans with plenty of *dodo* and *pomo*. I rashly uncorked the bottle of coca-cola and gulped its contents down my throat in one swoop. I gently raised the pillow and rested my back on it. It was not long afterwards that an instinct prompted me to leave the room. It was extremely sunny and the room was hot. The power had been out for almost two days leaving dusts to settle on the rickety ceiling fan that hung above me idly. Reluctantly, I stood up, took off my sweater and headed for the backyard.

At the backyard, I sat by the door opposite the State

Police Headquarters watching as trees were felled by contractors contracted to refurbish Ranchers Bees Stadium. Scattered around them were women mostly from the Police Barracks, waiting for the slightest opportunity to buy the trunks for both domestic and commercial purposes. This was peculiar of barracks lifestyle. Barracks women like *awoof*. Since the setting was like a community on its own, information flowed as to where to get cheap things. From cheap cooking ware to used clothes, to cheap food items, to cheap – anything!

From the gathering an argument ensued, followed by thunderous laughter. Behind the crowd, I saw mama gathering pieces of firewood scattered around, stacking them into a steel basin. She was sweltering from the shimmer of the sun.

'*Oga*, please sell that one to me', she pointed at a particular direction.

'Madam, that log is costlier than what you are bargaining', the man said in an accent that gave his identity away. He was a Hausa man. Knowing this, mama deployed her sixth sense into use.

'*Dan Allah ka taimake ni*, help me.' She pleaded in disjointed Hausa language, an attempt that betrayed her identity. She was from Kabba, a minority tribe in Kogi state. She brought out her leopard-skin pouch, unzipped it and stretched some pieces of rolled currency to him. For a moment, the man seemed lost as his eyes were fixated on a tree that was felled down.

'*Oya* bring what you have. But don't tell others how much I took from you.'

She would not tell anyone. It was a game she was quite familiar with. She thanked him.

For her size one would have thought she was frail but mama's unabated zeal to ensure we didn't starve was unequalled. Here was a woman who just had her seventh child barely eight months ago, after an experience that nearly cost her life. To some women, it would have meant total resignation to idleness. This and many other features were what must have prompted her husband sixteen years ago to ask for her hand in marriage. He knew she was dependable and that was why when the idea to go further his education in far away Katsina crossed his mind, he didn't find it hard to tell her.

It was at dinner after power outage. We were seated – six of us, round a bowl of pounded yam sending morsel after morsel down our throats when he hesitantly broke the news. There was grave silence then -

'What course and for how long?', mama had asked.

'Diploma in Criminology...' he responded intentionally avoiding the second question. He knew it would tear her apart considering the fact that she just gave birth to his last son barely three months ago.

'… rapid promotion and better life is what comes afterwards', he added with an intention to amuse her, but she was quiet and stolid. She was quiet for long and that bothered him.

'I want to give you and the children quality life. Things must not continue the way they are', he looked into her eyes. The glow of the lantern reflected in them. She heaved a heavy sigh and rested her back against the chair. She stretched her hand, picked a bowl of water within arm's reach and washed her hands, an evidence that she had lost appetite. It was obvious she was worried.

'When are you leaving?', she adjusted her sitting position.

'I just got the mail today', he avoided the question. He could discern she was bothered. But this is an opportunity he had waited for al his life. He had struggled to sit for the GCE exams and had passed all his papers. If he declined the admission offer, the entire essence of sitting for the exams in the first place would be fruitless. That he didn't want to settle for.

'You seem to be worried. If you don't want me to go, I can always decline the offer', it was an attempt at blackmail.

'Oh, why should I say that? This is what you have always wanted. My only concern is the children. How will I be able to cope with all of them? With you it was an arduous work getting them to assist with some of the house chores. What happens when you leave? Yes, I am worried. And only a responsible woman would. The last time you went on a course for three weeks, it was all hell loose. Now, who knows?' she asked rhetorically and before he said anything --

'You have not told me how long this will take', the words fell out of mama's mouth like a plea from a condemned prisoner requesting clemency. The silence that followed disturbed her. He looked at her and sniggered. He knew better than to tell her he was going to be away for two years. That was not the right moment. He would tell her when they were alone. At that moment a baby's cry stole into the silence from the single bedroom and startled all of us. It was Mohammed. He had woken up and must have noticed the absence of his mother. Mama swiftly rose to her feet and dashed into the bedroom. That was a relief from the tension that was mounting. I watched as father heaved a heavy sigh of relief. The rest was a story.

It's been almost a year since father left and mama had lived up to expectation. He had called a number of times through the office land phone and had related his mostly awful experiences to her on the phone. She had pitied him. On a particular day she came in moody after speaking with him on phone, which was unusual. She had always beamed with smiles each time she spoke with him. On asking why, she burst into tears. By the time she regained all composure to speak –

'Your father had nothing to eat and had soaked *garri* and *maggi* cube for dinner. It upset his stomach that he could not stand erect'. Initially I was in a dilemma of what appropriate response I should express. I had wanted to laugh it off. *Why would father take soaked garri and maggi cubes?*

Isn't that preposterous? I wondered. But the sullen look on mama's face coupled with the tears that snaked down my immediate younger sister's face took the better part of my emotions. It was then that the severity of the situation dawn on me. I pitied them. The following morning she gathered all the money she could from thrift to trade to borrowing, and sent it to him.

It was this and many more that crossed my mind before I fell asleep that evening only to wake to the probing eyes of the throng that gathered around me, attempting to revive me from my short journey elsewhere.

****

As I laid in the hospital bed that night, gazing at the rotating ceiling fan, I noticed uncle JJJ had rested his head on my bed, arms crossed, and dozed off. It must have been a tough day for him too. At this time the canaries had resigned into their respective nests. The night was serene save for the squeaking crickets and the altercating croak from the nearby toads. I listened as the symphony of the canaries ebbed out slowly.

I slept off.

It was the first call to prayer by the muezzin in a nearby mosque that woke me up the following morning. The shrill sound of the speakers was ear-piercing. My head pounded. Uncle JJJ was nowhere around. I managed to get up and lean my back against the pillow. An auxiliary nurse came in neatly dressed in a well -ironed blue gown, with a white belt round her waist, giving it befitting pleats on both sides. Her lips were glossed and her lashes darkened with mascara. Her aquiline nose was perfectly aligned with the symmetry of her body. She was slim.

'Good morning! How are you doing this morning? Please let's pray', she requested as if she was an automated answering machine – stereotyped. Her voice sounded more like a song than mere statement. She bowed her head in some form of reverence and began to pray.

It was about this time that mama entered the ward with a cooler and polythene bag in both hands, Mohammed strapped to her back. She smiled at me, closed her eyes and bowed as the prayer went on.

By the time the prayer was over, I opened my eyes and staring down at me were the nurse, uncle JJJ with a toothbrush in hand and mama.

'How is he?', mama asked uncle JJJ as she held my hand.

'Of course he is doing fine as you can see', the nurse responded with an assuring look on her face.

'He is doing fine', uncle JJJ responded forcing a grin.

But something was not right about the way he responded. There was silence in the meantime as the nurse took notes of progress report on a file.

'I'll be back', the nurse said. She smiled and vanished through a dual swinging door. Uncle JJJ and mama watched as she exited.

'Auntie, please let me see you for a minute', he held her by the arm.

'We will soon be back', uncle JJJ assured me before they vanished behind the doors. Something wasn't right but whatever that was I couldn't figure out at that moment. It was not long that mama returned. The brightness in her face when she entered the ward that morning was drowned by the somber mood she now wore. That confirmed by suspicion.

'What is it?', I managed to ask.

'We are leaving', she began to put my things together. That news gladdened my heart. I hated the sight of nurses carrying trays full of syringes and injections around. More so, I hated the slow-paced drip that hung somewhere above my head.

'Where is uncle?', I asked.

'He has gone to get a referral letter from the doctor and from there get a taxi', she dropped the bag she brought in earlier on the bed, unzipped it and stuffed it with my towel and sponge.

Referral letter? Does that mean we are leaving for another hospital? I wondered.

'Why?'

It was nothing she wanted to give an option of argument to, so she ignored me and continued packing.

'Are we going back home?'

The answer that came dwindled my earlier excitement.

'We are going to the General Hospital', mama said after a prolonged silence. Her eyes welled up in tears. She hid her face as she silently began to sing a song -

'Mo f'ija f'Olorun, mo f'owo leran…'

'Maa, are you crying?', It was a whisper. A few teardrops escaped from her eyes. She quickly turned her back at me.

'Am I going to die?'

'It is not your portion! Stop saying such things', she snarled as she turned and looked straight into my eyes. She managed to be strong, but the overwhelming mood betrayed her emotions. She was teary and her nose leaked. She resumed singing while folding my clothes.

I felt a pinch. The lyrics of that song gnawed at my heart. It was a song urging one to resign to fate. It was an assurance that when things fall apart and hopelessness crawls in, there is only one door left to knock on. I have heard her sing that song many times in the past, but it had never made sense to me like it did that morning. Those words came sharply with their intended tones and those tones brought alive their intended meaning. Lachrymose, I began to cry. Here was a woman with much vigour crushed to a mere feeble shadow of her former self worth.

****

It was not long before we arrived at the General Hospital that morning. I was familiar with the structures. Although I have admired the architectural designs from afar, I dreaded going near them. The hospital was situated some yards away from my school such that there was no way one could miss its elaborate sight when passing. On many occasions I have heard outcry and dirges from family members who lost their loved ones to the claws of death as I passed by the lonely windy road that led to my school. Aside those dirges, we have heard stories of ghosts hovering around the hospital premises, haunting. I have had goose pimples on some occasions. I have suspected everybody that went in or out of the structures as walking corpses. And of course there were many visitors , among which were loved ones who came by the road side to buy fruits from the women displaying their wares in front of the hospital gate. I once had an experience on a particular day I was late to school. The road was deserted and from behind me I heard a voice.

'Can you part with some coins?' it was a female's voice. I quickly turned to look at the haggard-looking figure seated by the foot of a guava tree. There was no option but *one*. My legs' decision was in tandem with my instincts. I never knew I was such a good sprinter until that afternoon. I ran as fast I could as if the entirety of my life depended on it.

'I will never go to school late again', I resolved after I had reached the giant gate of my school, where students were lined up by the Disciplinary Officer for appropriate punishment.

At least this is a lesser punishment compared to my earlier encounter. I had thought as I joined the file of errant students.

Today, the taxi zoomed past the gate of these same structures, and pulled over before a storey building. It was painted sap blue. Before the taxi revved to a stop, the door to the building flung open and four auxiliary nurses in sparkling white gowns rushed out with a stretcher. Behind those four nurses was uncle JJJ, who had earlier on alighted from the taxi as soon as we got to the gate. He was going to see how to hasten up things before our arrival.

'There he is', uncle JJJ pointed towards my direction.

The auxiliary nurses adroitly placed the stretcher near the car door and lifted me onto it. I had struggled to see if I could do that on my own, but all effort was futile. My limbs were numb and my head ached acutely. I was stretchered into a ward with lined up beds on either side. There were over thirty beds in the ward. It was crowded. As we passed by the aisle, repulsive stench of drug mixtures greeted my nose. On the first bed to my left was a child with mucus dangling from his nose who had refused to be fed by his worried mother. He had shoved all attempts and had spilled the pap on the bed. The mother had pleaded with him to at least take some. On the second bed to my left was a scraggy looking patient with a tube attached to his penis for urinal purpose. His eyes were bulging out of their sockets, and his cheeks looked chiseled. His mouth was ajar, exposing his discoloured dentures to the buzzing flies around. One would have thought he was dead if not for the occasional rise and fall of his lower abdomen. A woman sat beside the bed fanning away the flies with her wrapper. She looked at me as we passed by, and shook her head pitifully. I turned to my right and on the fourth bed to my right, near an alternate exit, was a chubby man of mid fifties sitting with a newspaper in his hand. He looked healthy. His ebony skin was lush. He wore a smile as we passed by nodding his head in our direction. On a seat near him was a Mobile Police officer holding a walkie-talkie and on his waist was a holstered pistol.

We soon arrived at an empty bed. It was at this time that I *slept* off.

By the time I woke up, there were vague images of several nurses in white coveralls around my bedside each with a notepad and a pen in hand. A stout man with thick well-trimmed moustache stood in front of them as they scribbled points. The bed was barricaded by a thin fabric sheet, giving me some right of privacy. I searched around for my mother, but she was nowhere near. Neither was uncle JJJ. Some chill passed through my skin. It was not until then that I discovered I was naked. I tried to utter some words, but my words were incoherent. My head pounded.

'He is suffering from Cerebrospinal meningitis which causes acute convulsive reflexes', the stout man said to the nurses.

The name of that illness sounded smooth as they escaped from his lips. *Why is it that acute illnesses always have smooth names?* I wondered.

'What causes such?' a female nurse standing by the foot of the bed asked.

'Heat. Too much exposure to heat', the stout man answered while tapping his note pad with a finger. He continued, 'Any other question?' it was then he discovered I was awake.

'Mikail, how are you feeling?'

'Fine', I managed to answer. It was a lie. My head was pounding but there was no how I could express it since my speech organ was in temporal dysfunction.

'His words will be incoherent at the moment due to drug infusion, but he should recover in no time. So, at intervals, ensure you load him with xxx drugs to stabilize him. He possibly might not know when the attack comes because it usually seems like a short sleep', this he said to his student nurses.

He turned to look at me.

'I am Dr. Ahmed Ali and these are my colleagues in the profession.'

Is he for real? How could he do such an introduction when he knew I was disadvantaged by my nakedness? I had thought. The nurses smiled at me. I knew what was going on in their minds especially the ladies amongst them. Even when it was time for them to leave, some of them scanned my form again to keep the image of what they saw intact in their memory. I was ashamed of that surreal episode. After the doctor and his student nurses left that evening, my eyes curiously searched through my bed space. A sachet of injection water hung over my head supplying fluids to my body through a needle affixed to my vein. In the trashcan near the headrest were used syringes and empty injections containers.

When were these used? How come I did not feel the pains of injections? What sort of illness is this? My mind kept probing for answers. Just about then, the curtains parted slightly. Mama peeped through.

'*Oluwa Ose*! Thank you Lord! *Pele*... sorry', she stretched her hands heavenwards and let go of the curtains. Mama and uncle JJJ had earlier on been instructed to stay outside the ward by the resident doctor, after I had a seizure. This I later got to know.

By 9.00 pm, silence settled in as visitors were led out of the ward. The moon was perfectly round and the stars bright in their scattered formation. The amber security light contributed to the luminous that lit the distant streets. Everything seemed naturally normal until the thudding feet of some auxiliary nurses stormed the ward in quick succession. Doctor Ali was in tow.

'Fix the oxygen...', he said as he approached the ebony man.

'Yes sir!' a male nurse replied, unpacking equipment from a toolbox.

'It's too late', Doctor Ali said with an air of finality.
A nurse pulled out a white piece of cloth from a polythene bag and covered the dark-skinned man. He was immediately stretchered out of the ward.

'Just like that?' the mobile police officer, who now stood by himself asked as he shook his head. 'He was a good man... My boss was a good man.' It was rather a consolation monologue than it was an accolade.

'How could one who seemed as healthy as he did die just like

that? I had wondered.

'What happened to him?' I asked mama.

'He is being taken to a new ward since he has fully recovered', uncle JJJ quickly interrupted before mama could utter a word. I sniggered. I had seen through uncle JJJ's euphemistical attempt to dissuade me from the reality of the moment. I sure understood his position judging by the very factor that the high ranking police officer who just passed on had the same ailment as mine. This I later got to know through the rumour-mill.

'Uncle, I know he is dead. But of what?', I asked giving him no option to argue further.

The second part of the question was obviously hard for him to respond to either. He smiled.

'What will you do with what ailment killed him, if you were told?', mama queried. I shrugged and dispelled further questions.

The following morning was Saturday and that accounted for the discordant noise that filled the space of the ward. Visitors were allowed in to see their patients. Among these visitors were some church members who thronged around the child I had passed by the day before praying fervently. Then an outbreak of outcry followed. It was the child's mother.

'His feet are cold...' she said and dashed out. The prayer session immediately halted and a grave silence followed. A moment later the mother of the child and two nurses returned.

'Excuse us please', one of the nurses pleaded while ushering the visitors out. The other nurse checked for the child's pulse and shook her head.

'Sorry, he is gone!'

The mother broke into uncontrollable wailing as the child was stretchered out. My heart pounded as I witnessed the unfolding of that event. I had never seen a dead body before, but here I was in the space of just a couple of hours experiencing, two in a row. I was frightened. The officer's death was not as frightening and as emotional as that of the child. I was brooding over this when I heard my name from the right bedside.

'Mikail… he is dead?'

It was Lucas: a patient who had swollen stomach for eight weeks from not defecating. His belly was round and shiny. He was thin. It was said that his ailment was as a result of some spiritual attack. I had, out of fear, consciously avoided eye contact with him ever since I was admitted. Now it was a reality I had to contend with. I ignored him, silently praying that mama and uncle JJJ would return in time to save the day. That never happened, at least not so soon.

'May the Lord repose his soul and give us good health, Mikail my friend', Lucas consoled.

I gently turned to look at his side. His eyes were closed.

'Ameen', I responded silently.

That response, as if anticipated, led to a long discourse as Lucas opened up and told me the entire episode of how he landed in the sick bed. He was a straight 'A' student aspiring to be a pilot someday. He had just been enlisted in an Airforce Academy on a state scholarship, a path towards actualizing his dreams. He had resumed school and study was underway when he observed he had malaria symptoms. It was after all efforts by the Academy clinic proved unyielding ,that he was accompanied home for proper medical attention.

'I eat voraciously but cannot defecate…', he chuckled and continued, 'The world is wicked Mikail…human beings are cruel.'

I heaved a deep sigh and shook my head. The discussion was laid to rest after mama and uncle JJJ returned to the ward from where they went to get some fruits for me.

My relationship with Lucas grew stronger in the proceeding weeks as we discussed issues – social, political, academic and any other thing that was the subject matter. The time was 10:15 pm when Lucas asked Uncle JJJ.

'Please let me know when it is 12.00 a.m. I mean midnight', Lucas pleaded with Uncle JJJ. My uncle nodded to his request.

'What will you be doing midnight?', Lucas' mother who was seated by his bed quickly asked.

'Prayers', he responded with a soft demeanour.

His mother walked up to my uncle and muttered some words to him. They were discussing alongside mama when I slept off.

'Lucas! Lucas!', it was Lucas's mother's shrill voice. It tore through my dreamland and forcefully jerked me out of sleep. I turned to look at Lucas. He was chest-pumping. Uncle JJJ quickly ran out and returned with Dr. Ali. Soon the curtains was used to partition Lucas' bed space as nurses rally round giving all form of medical attention. It was time. It was exactly a minute past 12.00 a.m.

****

The day after Lucas' demise was full of encouraging words from mama. I had wept all night and my head had pounded continuously. That night I presumed I was going to die. I thought the ward was for those on the waiting list of death. A sort of gateway to a place of no return! I encountered four gruesome deaths. Death picking ages at random!

****

Today, I looked at mama's failing health and began to cry as my heart scribbles...

Last night I was at your bed's foot
watching you sleep in strange weakness.
Your ebony skin drooped, folding
into countless ageing wrinkles.
I counted those wrinkles –

they are the number of my years.

I looked at the flip-flop like flesh
that now represents your robust bosom –
same I've suckled for growth and life,
tears rumbled behind my eyes.

I know one day…
I'll search the barn, hut and farm; where
you've labored to make me whole,
only echoes of your past will linger
between the Almond trees.

Where is your valour
that once rode on hyenas and cheetahs?

How so much time has sapped
the enchantments of your youth!

Maami, I dread the day I foresee –
the day when your limbs will grow cold
and the earth devours you in its chilling warmth!

Rasheed Adewusi

Rasheed Adewusi holds a B.A (Hons) from the prestigious Obafemi Awolowo University, Ile-Ife. He is currently running an MBA Programme from the same Institution. He is an avid reader and likes to refer to himself as "an information glutton". He loves Scrabble, Football, Basketball, and Movies.

He is a Sales Manager in one the telecommunication companies operating in Nigeria. He is married with a kid. His personal ambition is to immeasurably contribute to making the world a better place than he met it; and his personal mantra is "Do your best, and continue to do the rest."

He is very visible on social media - @SirRash, Rasheed SirRash Adewusi, , and personally runs the blog *Wise, Wide and Wild*

RESTLESS IN THE SHADE

It is Monday morning, the sun is up, Friday joins millions of other Lagosians to troop onto the roads in search of their daily bread. As is the norm with him anytime he is not with people he is familiar with, Friday starts musing about Lagos roads on Monday mornings – they are like the rainbow, not in its colourful or renewing state, but in its state of not knowing when it started and when it will go away. Some are pushing and shoving with their hands and bodies, while others have employed their automobiles to achieve exactly the same objective. It is pretty impossible to find someone who is solely responsible for all the aggression and foul mood on Lagos roads on Mondays, but we can all blame it on "time", that phenomenon which has a way of not slowing down, let alone stop, when we choose to be inactive.

Friday is thirty-two years old. He lives in Apapa. He works in Ikeja. We can call him a walking documentary of the hardship on Lagos roads, because he has lived it for fourteen years. He moved to Lagos from Agbor after completing his secondary education and since then, he has been moving from one odd job to the other. He had worked as a bar-attendant, a yoghurt hawker, a laundry assistant, a hotel cleaner, among other jobs. If resumés were actually needed for the kind of jobs he gets, Friday's resumé will be about twenty-pages long. At the moment, his uniform has "Facility Manager" emblazoned on its back, but he is not more than an 'office cleaner'. His daily routine involves making sure the offices are swept and mopped; the chairs, tables, desks, and computers are dusted and polished; the toilets are cleaned, shined and have tissue papers, air-fresheners, and handwash liquid; he is practically responsible for the cleanliness of the whole office environment. He also runs errands like buying food and washing cars for the office staff . These chores he carries out with a smile on his face and his back straight. John has come to accept his place in the office and he revels in his position as the go-to man for petty errands. Of course, he also gets some little 'change' here and there, but those are not equal to his ebullience and enthusiasm. However, he is not the only Facility Manager in the office complex; there are two others – Blessing and Chukwudi, popularly known as Chuks.

Blessing is a thirty-six year old efik lady . She lives in Itire. She works in Ikeja. She is married with two kids. She moved to Ikot- Ekpene to Lagos with her husband, five years ago. Her husband has worked for many years in the construction industry and decided to move to Lagos with his family with the hope of getting a job as a foreman, convinced his wealth of experience coupled with the number of construction projects going on all around Lagos, provides him the right platform to achieve his aim. Blessing therefore left her wholesale beer business and moved to Lagos, full of hope and filled with dreams. Lagos welcomed them with open arms, embraced them with its hostility of accommodation, its bile of mobility, and swallowed them into its bowel of perpetual hustling. The foreman job did not materialize and Blessing's husband continued to work as a labourer around Ikoyi; Blessing had to get a job with one of the "facility managing" firms around. Blessing is in charge of the upper floor of the complex while Friday mans the ground floor.

Chuks is what you can call a typical Lagos Island Boy. Though he hails from Nnewi, he was born and raised in Lagos. His lifestyle smirks of the outlandish and fun-seeking tendencies that are trademarks of the people of *Isale Eko*. He is twenty-three years old. Having completed his secondary school education, he lacked the requisite result to proceed to a higher institution of learning but dreams of owning a Bugatti someday; albeit he was devoid of the roadmap on how to achieve that. He was compelled to work with the facility managing firm by his elder brother when he got out of control and could easily pass for a miscreant at Ojuelegba. His host had threatened to hand him over to his soldier friend for some straightening, if he does not desist from being a scoundrel. His friends in the neighbourhood do not know he is practically an office cleaner because he leaves home in the morning dressed in trendy t-shirts or classy shirts thrown over a pair of baggy jeans, not forgetting to lace a nice pair of Timberland boots or Converse sneakers; all these are supplied by his 'clothier' who runs a 'bend- down boutique' at one of the stalls on the fringe of the rail track at Yaba As a 'street boy', he knows how to 'look fly' at low cost..

In the office, you will never find Chuks frolicking with the other facility managers because he was seconded to those parts of the building where only the *Ogas* frequent; rather his posting brings him in contact with the executives and managers who find it easy to socialize with him because of his demeanor.

In addition to his duties as a facility manager, Chuks also made it part of his call to engage customers as they come into the office, such that he fast-tracks their requests for a token. Patrons have come to accept that when it comes to procuring 'through-the-back-door' merchandise, there is no better point man than Chuks.

The Manager of the office complex, Mr Sanjo Ayinde, is a very introspective man whose life story will be a very interesting read if he were to summon the courage to write or commission a ghost writer for an autobiography. He grew up in a household where having anything at all was a luxury. He practically sponsored himself through secondary school as well as the university. Being very resourceful, he was able to augment his university education through scholarships, bursaries, and hand- outs he got from his classmates, whom he helped with assignments and tutorials. He knew what it was to aspire without having the material support, but his desire, determination, and dedication to get out of the doldrums got him to where he is today.

Each day he came to the office, SJ as he is fondly called, looked at and analysed the mien and body language of the three facility managers, and secretly prayed that someday, one of them would come to him with a grand plan that has his aspiration as its crux; but that day may never come as all his subordinates clamour for is to be the first to say "Good Morning Sir" and rush to grab his bag. He kept affording them the luxury hoping that would get them close enough to him to seek his help in any form. On a certain day, he decided to call them all and wring out their future plans from them, hoping against hope that they would have some. He needed to do that as quickly as possible. He decided he had to do it today.

SJ called the three facility managers into his office and told them he is having a little get-together for friends in his house on Sunday, and he would like them all to be there. They were so elated and promised t not to miss it. He further stressed that the invitation was exclusive to them , they need not bring anyone, including members of their family, along, as he is working with a shoestring budget. They all assented and thanked him profusely before taking their leave from his office.

On Sunday, the trio of Friday, Blessing, and Chuks, all gaily dressed, arrived at SJ's house before the agreed time of two in the afternoon; if there had been other guests of SJ's social status, these three would still have fit in perfectly.

SJ, casually dressed in a plain collared t-shirt over a knee-length combat shorts and a pair of leather slippers, was so happy to see them and welcomed them enthusiastically, no airs. He offered them refreshments according to their respective tastes, after which called his family, consisting of his wife and two daughters, for a proper introduction. He made them feel valued and welcome. SJ never stopped apologizing: ' lunch will soon be served please'. He made sure they felt at home.

Food, in the form of Poundo Yam and Egusi Soup, garnished with assorted meat, fish, stockfish and periwinkles, was eventually served around fifteen minutes past three. Once they had their fill, SJ, hinted that "real drinks " will soon follow for those who are loyalists of Bacchus, and left the table with his family promising to be back at exactly four o'clock.

At this stage, the trio began to wonder when other guests would arrive, but Blessing, being a bold person, voiced her confusion to her two colleagues. Friday responded that they were probably operating with African time; but Chuks in his usual manner snapped at the other two asking what business of theirs it is if others were early or not. He further rebuked them for not being happy that they came early and had the best part of the food, aside from enjoying the 'oyinbo movies' on DSTV. He rounded off. with a long hiss to show his disdain for their level of reasoning.

At exactly four o'clock, SJ finally came into the living room, turned off the television , and proceeded to set the air conditioner at optimal temperature. He then sat on a double seat and asked his three guests to occupy the sofa which could comfortably seat three persons at a time.

He started by welcoming them once again asking if they were enjoying themselves, or if they wanted anything else. In turn, they expressed their satisfaction. SJ, adjusting himself in his seat, finally broke the ice: there was no party whatsoever, he only invited them so he could have a heart-to-heart talk with them.

He told them of his pain each time he saw them around the office, acting as if they had reached their preferred destinations in life. He moved to the edge of his seat and continued.' I salute your disposition towards your duties, I must say you are completely devoted to you various assignments. However, such energy should be invested in better and more lofty goals. Life is not static, thus you should not.' Seeing he had their full attention, he became more relaxed and asked that each one intimate him on his or her past, present and most importantly, plans for the future To make sure they were at ease to discuss such personal stuff with him, he proceeded to share his bit first.

Sanjo was born into a polygamous family in the late Seventies. His father had four wives and fourteen children of which SJ is the third of five children from his own mother. The father was a carefree man who considered himself a gift to womenfolk and was never shy of giving himself out to any woman who would have him. Catering to the needs of the children that resulted from those dalliances never crossed his mind, and projecting himself as a model for his children was one luxury he could not afford. Growing up in Lagos Island in the Eighties, Sanjo could not particularly pinpoint what his father did for a living, but he knew that occasionally, he used to come home with a lot of money which he squandered on women and drinks faster than the money had come. In retrospection, he had no role model in his father, and his older siblings were too busy fending for themselves to mentor anyone.

Continuing his story, he recalled that the streets of Lagos Island were rife with crime and drug abuse and if he had to make something of his life, he knew he had to take the bull by the horn. He focused on his studies and ensured he finished his secondary education. But the dream of going further to a university looked far-fetched and his mother at that point was not the healthiest of women having endured the stress of raising five children all by herself. He did not want to go into petty trading because the people all around him either got swindled or had their houses burgled. He could not go into crime and drug-peddling because he had seen enough lives end abruptly as a result of involvement in drugs. He felt he had no other option except to use his natural gift – his intelligence.

This was the Nineties, when Tutorial Centres sprung up and became the fad. He therefore relocated to Yaba, set-up a tutorial center with three other like-minded friends, and started putting out word that they could help people pass all forms of examinations from WAEC to GCE, IAMB etc,. Of course, that was just a front for an outfit which specialized in acting as mercenaries for people who wanted to pass such examinations but do not have the mental aptitude to, or who were simply lazy. Being a very brilliant chap, his track record started speaking for him and his fame began to spread. With the proceeds of his new venture, he was able to send himself through the university. Courtesy of his high intelligence, he got scholarships, bursaries, and in addition, made money from helping his classmates with tutorials and their assignments. He graduated with a First Class Degree in Business Administration. This got him a plum job in a multi-national company and he has been moving up the Corporate ladder ever since.

Looking back, he said, he is not at all proud of his past. He would not have plied that route, but when he considers that five of his fourteen siblings are dead from complications resulting from drug abuse and indiscriminate sex; another two in jail for engaging in criminal activities; while another two are still treading the path of crime, he always felt he took the right decision to get to where he is presently. By the way, he later found out that his father was a drug trafficker. He was assassinated by his associates when their business relationship turned awry. His father, Adepate, had informed his partners in crime that his big dream is to float his own company within the next five years and his area of focus would be software development. He would float an NGO to nurture young minds with aptitude for technology to achieve their full potentials. His co- peddlers would have none of such plans as they could not bear to lose Adepate, who had a Midas touch in selling drugs.

Blessing who is usually reluctant to speak was the first to respond, and she was doing so with a shaky voice, hinting that she was fighting back tears. She said that she had always believed that she is just an appendage to her husband ; that once her husband is successful, she is successful. She also revealed that she has considered Lagos as a place where she cannot fit in and that leaving the house every morning for the office complex is a form of escapism for her. She revealed that she has a great aptitude for buying and selling, but that the belief that her husband will soon get a job a foreman has totally made her not to consider putting her strengths to use. She submitted that she had just been existing but not living, at which point she started weeping uncontrollably. SJ had to get her some tissue paper to wipe her tears. In-between the sobs, she started asking what would happen to her if her husband suddenly starts misbehaving or even if he dies untimely (God forbid), and the weeping increased. At this point , SJ had to get her a glass of water to calm her frayed nerves and assured her all would be well. Finally, she expressed her resolve to open an account with a Microfinance Bank and start contributing towards reviving her beer business, not minding the size.

Chuks, the ebullient chap, crouched in a corner like a puppy that has just been rescued from a bucket of chilled water. He further said that his dream has always been to travel out of the country; he has no particular destination in mind, and he has no roadmap or timeline to achieve the objective. But he believes that when the time is right, it will happen like magic!. He said he has never for once given a thought to going to a higher institution, and while he is here, he has no plans of engaging in any tangible business or learning any craft because he does not see his future here. He confessed he had only floated through life but he has come to realize how stupid he had been all this while, living with neither a plan nor a timeline. He intimated SJ of his decision to register for the next WASSCE, and also to enroll for training on telephone and laptop repairs in his spare time.

Friday claimed he always had dreams but his position as the foremost 'Facility Manager' in the office complex, coupled with the kind of fantastic relationship he enjoys with almost everybody, have deceived him into thinking he is comfortable the way he is. He simply revealed that his dream is to float his own laundry business which he expects to grow into general cleaning ; his handicap has been finance.

Expectedly, the three august guests at this point had grabbed the full import of what SJ was driving at. They never realized that they were selling themselves short. They all came to the conclusion that their past is not responsible for their current situation; rather it is their decision to allow their past loom so large as to overshadow their future.

'Tobi Adebowale

'Tobi was born in Lagos in 1989. He is a final year Law student at the Obafemi Awolowo University, Ile-Ife and an Associate Mediator. He writes mostly on social and political issues expressed through poetry, fiction and non-fiction.

He has been published on many platforms like Saraba, The Guardian and many more. He is a weekly political columnist at www.thescoopng.com and keeps a personal blog at tobisammyjay.wordpress.com. He also runs a literature interactive platform, Writers Discourse Group.

A TRACE OF BLOOD

NOW I can tell what it feels like to live without it all, the shoes and shirts and shocks of life but most of all, I miss my pen. I simply hover around now, clasping my palms upon my ears, wishing I had enough wax in there to cushion the sounds. I have had to watch so many reviews of life, of the sad and the bad, the light and the bright, even of mine that comes with a date-tag of February 14. The clip begins at the worship centre, blinding colours of headgear filling up the pews and sonorous tones climbing to the roof from the choir at the right corner, their garments red as blood.

I come up at the entrance of Cortland Gardens, my wife and child on my tail, beside many other celebrants of the sun's demise trooping in. It was the first time we had decided to hang out in four years. We marched calmly towards a bench, careful enough to avoid the band of young men locked in binge drinking. Hadley beer was free for as many who took time to get to the truck. I laughed within; I had done the same things many years before walking down the aisle.

Laura gave me the same look that had dragged me to her many years back at a bar in Enugu, just this time, she was my wife asking for a dance. My hands settled on her waist as we ambled to the centre, swaying to the music. The smell of her hair took me to the office. Sheila had a similar smell that afternoon as we dissolved in passion, shoving aside my editorial on the latest fuel scarcity in the country, and when she left, she wore a smile that seemed more pregnant than my heavy cousin.

If I had the rights, I would have stopped the review of my life when it got to the part where Laura and I went completely immersed in our world, sealed up in the heavy beats from the disc jockey. The seconds sped though, like fleeing rats. It was the moment four men showed up, all huge and daring. The first shoved me aside with what seemed of no effort to him.

"I want a dance with her," he bellowed.

"No way, that's my wife," I replied.

Watching it now helps to fill in the unconscious moments that followed our two-minute heated debate. Silver metals shining under the dim light appeared from the other three. One lodged his in my belly, the next in my shoulder and the third in my chest. Then they went in quick turns around every part of my body they wanted and thought appealing, the screams of my wife drowned by the flashes of silver and the sputter of blood. In six heavy steps they were out of the Gardens, commotion and curdling blood on their trail; my eyelids close in half and faintly I hear an attendant's gripe about bloodstains on the dance floor, well over my wife's persistent calls.

Josh interrupts my life's review with a thump on his chest where the tear into his breast is yet to heal. He points at a figure from his life review, and I pause mine to see Josh thrust through in the chest by a dirty Caucasian on a rowdy Harlem street. They had been arguing over a missing condom pack in a run-down apartment they shared with six other men. Josh brings the timeline to the point where he had thumped his chest and I see shiny courtrooms, contrasting sharply with Josh's dingy neighbourhood. The judge, Ms. Fairclough reads from a paper, her spectacles sinking upon her nose as she pronounced a one-way trip to the electric chair for the dirty Caucasian.

Adebolu arrives as the credits on Josh's earth panorama begin to roll, his eyes squinting at the enormous lighting that surrounded us. It's easy to tell that he is from my homeland having experienced similar discomfiture upon my arrival. He limps towards me. I turn towards my screen to see scruffy cops rounding up jolly-goers at Cortland Gardens. I recall the countless editorials bled out from my pen about the Police, their incompetence, nonchalance and occasional extra-judicial fervency. I was caught in-between rejoicing that arrests were being made over an incident in which I have earned the victim tag, and lamenting the manhandling of many innocent party-goers over the same. I looked away, looking up to see what the new Editor will write about the arrests.

Adebolu's screen is being set up ;when I look away from my screen, his attention firmly rested on Josh's screen who seemed to delight in seeing a review of his last review for the umpteenth time. When Adebolu looked away, I recognized the look in his face, a common bout of solidarity flu that made us sneeze away any hope of enjoying same pleasures as Josh. We may never see our actual predators given same treatment as they were sure to get in Josh's country, we knew it and we knew there was little we could do about it from this side. To the system and its beneficiaries, we were mere traces of existence, not worthy of half-masts or days of mourning. When by their often cluelessness, they are plucked from the skies to their early deathbeds, they were super-humans worthy of immortality, not us, mere traces of blood.

REDEMPTION

Mechi

A cloud of darkness descended on Mechi as the massive gate locks of the Ijebu-Ode maximum prison clasped behind him. A blend of sweat and heat mixed with the air that wafted into his nostrils, as his eyes rolled from one end of the walls to another just three feet away and at least six warders in khaki in-between. The cuffs on his wrists seemed to tighten at will, yet he feared to ask the lead warder with the key to let his hands free. He couldn't afford another half-hour tongue-lashing as he had experienced in times past. The enveloping darkness acquired more thickness. As they arrived at Cell D, his home since twelve months; the gates opened to a stretch of sixteen-by-six-feet room, two near-roof windows, twelve cold faces and a waving buba[1] held by Kamoru whose turn it was to fan President. The officer behind retrieved a key from his waist-band and unlocked Mechi's handcuffs, giving him a slight shove into the cell that could be confused with a pat on the back, only the smirk on his lips was sinister. He hailed President and turned away humming.

"*Odaran[2] banker, you don come,*" President thundered. He had been there longer than anyone else. An overlord. He enjoyed the thrill of holding court in the cell and

---

[1] Upper garment worn by the Yoruba people of South-West Nigeria
[2] Yoruba word for criminal

punishing anyone as he deemed fit, particularly those who slacked while taking their turn to fan him, his exclusive privilege.

Mechi staggered to the far end of the cell opposite President's throne-end. He knew any of the other eleven inmates could land him a blow at President's command but it was more reassuring to be far from the thundering demon himself. Scars lined up President's arms even up to his right knuckles. The sight of the scars drew a bitter taste from Mechi's empty belly to his mouth. He remembered them. He remembered them very well.

On his arrival at the cell eighteen months earlier, President was known then as Speaker while a short tougher-looking inmate with a bulging tummy called Leke presided over the cell. Speaker came to him and ordered him to remove his shirt, and then his vest and then his trousers. He graced Mechi's face with a deafening slap the moment he hesitated and a blow to his tummy when he tried to question him. By his face and weight, he couldn't be older than twenty-five, at least ten years younger than him, Mechi thought to himself but he soon realized that was a distant consideration to Speaker when he finally obeyed. Speaker snapped his fingers in the air and like a deluge, six other inmates charged at Mechi as a bull would at the sight of his red boxers. He arched his back to dodge a kick headed for his belly but another kick from the rear ensured he opened up to receive the portions of his "baptism" meant for his belly. Hard and dirty knuckles took turns around his face, arms, chest and every part he could helplessly not shield. When they were done, Speaker read the ten cell commandments to him above his drooping head and swollen face, his eyes counting the scars on Speaker's legs, of their own will. He trailed many more scars to his chest and neck and in his woozy brain filled with many stars, he concluded the man must have been in many bottle-and-knife fights. His thought lingered on the knife part, flickered and passed out, his wrecked soul almost wriggling out of his tired body, a pitiable mass on the concrete floor. He woke up to a watery pottage and sachet water which the goons next to him urged him to hurry up. It was time for Leke to deliver his presidential welcome slap and hand over the buba for the night. He fanned Leke till he slept and when his hands went numb, he sat down and rested his back on the wall, next to Toyota, a thin inmate who scratched his groin in his sleep. The warders turned up one morning to take Leke away, arms and legs chained. He never returned, only differing stories of his conviction for kidnapping and ritual killing or for armed robbery and murder.

Mechi took a deep breath as he pulled off his shirt and adjusted to the heat. Sights and sounds of the grueling cross-examination earlier played in a gripping reel in his mind. Abraham Mokuro, Esq. had a great time drilling him, asking every wild question his imagination could come up with. All the minutes Mechi's defence counsel, Chudi Okafor spent preparing him seemed to amount to little the very moment Mokuro began to pressure him to describe the last days of Clara, his wife, up to the moment when she breathed her last in their bedroom.

Clara

Mechi turned on the left side of the bed, his chosen side since the first night of his marriage to Clara on May 26th 2007. Clara sighed as she gazed at his eyes. He was just a feet away from her but all day long, on their fifth wedding anniversary, more than a kilometer seemed to be wedged in-between them. He gave her no roses and cakes as he had done on their first anniversary or even a tersely addressed greeting card like he grudgingly dropped on her laps a few months back on Valentine's Day. Her right fingers went up, crawling in the air towards his face, her mind undecided about how to say what she wanted to say. She had questions for him but she was not angry, she was tired of that. On their fifth wedding anniversary, Mechi left the house in a pink shirt and his grey suit, the blue crest of his employers tagged to his left lapel, just above his chest. It made her jealous. She thought of the days Mechi placed her lean fingers on that left part of his chest and assured her she would always have a place there. Now, it seemed wearing a bank lapel was the only thing the chest was made for. He left for work without saying a word, perhaps he had exhausted the quota for the day while they argued the night before. The time was well past 11pm when he returned and still having no words for her, simply climbed unto his side of the bed as though in a hurry to catch up with a fast-slipping sleep. She watched him, studied the gratified look on his face as he snored more heavily by the second. Anger had gradually eased itself out for care since the days he openly told her she was frigid and that he was getting it elsewhere. It was their fifth anniversary and she was not angry that they had been angry at each other for four straight days, or at the smell of another woman that jumped at her from him, she only cared to know if he was satisfied. She was surprised at her thoughts and at how much she wanted to ask him if he had used protection. She dropped her hands and muttered to herself, *"You had a great day at work, happy anniversary"*.

Morning came and Clara surprised herself by making him breakfast for the first time in a week. Like forlorn kids, the bread and eggs sat on his plate at the table, untouched and attacked by the cold air but he managed to say "thanks" on his way out of the flat. She nodded in response. It was 6am and soon the rev of his car just behind their bedroom cut through the silence of dawn and through the thick fog of confusion that stretched across the firmaments of her mind. There was a crack of light at the end and still images of mornings when they dissolved in passion, the time he liked it best, and then of glorious sunsets when he serenaded her with sonnets written on bank memo pads. They came to him at work. She longed for the fullness of that light, again.

Titi was Clara's chief bridesmaid at her wedding to Mechi, her friend and confidant with a capsule for every issue. Titi's desk was her first point of call on arriving at Adebambo & Co., the auditing firm where she worked as a data analyst. Titi told her it was a thorny path all couples walked through before reaping their roses, she had been there before and they could discuss further at lunch. The clock took its time to move from then on, too much time in Clara's estimation. There was little left to do for her by noon but lunch was still a full hour away. She opened a new window on her computer , logged into her twitter account and posted a quote from Zig Ziglar. It spoke to her heart more than it did anyone else but she felt good putting it up. It was therapeutic. She got sixteen retweets, one of them from @mainmanmechi. It made her smile, even though she wondered why she should have. She clicked his handle and read briefly through his timeline. He talked about thieving politicians, disloyal friends and his favorite football team, Barcelona. Nothing caught her fancy until she scrolled to the last tweet full of political innuendoes. She clicked on the conversation and read through. It dripped of Mechi's sense of humour, the one she had always known, the one that won her over at the NYSC orientation camp. She checked on Dark Duchess' profile. Mechi was probably one of the many men she was exchanging political jokes and laughter emoticons with, only that Clara could sense some emotional balloon hanging over his conversation with her. It didn't add to what she already knew, of his new philandering ways and his revolving bata[3]-like temperament that turned its cacophonous side towards her more than it played soothing melodies to other women.

Titi probed Clara about her sex life then gave a few hints. They worked for a friend who fell apart with her

---

[3] Bata is an African drum with two opposing ends

husband, and for another friend who needed to get her man to propose. Clara could not tell if she was grateful. Mechi, like other men as her late mother used to tell her, were stars astronomers always ascribed different attributes. Mechi was always sweet, always different from other men she had been with in the university up until the third year of their marriage when his mother's persistent yells about their seemingly fruitless marriage began to form creases on his forehead. She wanted to raise the Dark Duchess' lengthy Twitter conversation while she talked with Titi, but it somewhat evaded attention, like bright meteors flashing across the night into a dark end. Titi mentioned seeing a counselor and she agreed with her. It was perhaps about time. She also wanted her to try a novena, perhaps the feisty influences luring Mechi away and constantly springing up heated debates with him will dissipate into thin air, and pave way for a deep connection of their souls. It should be easier to conceive if they were sheathed by such divine harmony when they were under the sheets.

Two days after her visit to Father Moses with Titi and a session with the resident counselor at the parish, Mechi returned home from the City Sports Club where he had gone to meet with a few friends. It was a part of his weekend routine to hang out with friends in different parts of town. They rocked the Club dance floor together on Friday nights while they were dating but not anymore. He smiled at her as she opened the door, an unnerving stretch across his face. It was very close to his saintly smiles in the years when he drank with moderation, when he cuddled her in the evenings and assured her he would stand by her always, up until the first sunny afternoon he dazed her a hot slap for daring to disrespect his mother. Mama Mechi maintained a non-interference policy in her son's life choices but all that changed when her yearning for omugwo[4] overtook her patience. She turned up at Mechi's

---

[4] Igbo word for babysitting by mothers-in-law

home with potency charms for him and barrage of insults for his wife, riling Clara to the point of helpless disgust.

"My mom is coming over," he seemed excited as he said the words. His smile was to mock her, to prepare the ground for her tormentor-in-chief. She decided to prove him wrong. She smiled in return and added a hug though it seemed more like embracing an electric pole. The novena had to be working, it had to work, it was meant to work, she reiterated in her mind.

Caro

Caro symbolized everything Mechi fantasized about. It began as a suggestion from his passionate mother then Tade and John asked why he was slow at giving it a trial. They were not exactly in his shoes, with a kid each, they kept mistresses just for the thrill of it. They introduced him to Onome while they downed bottles of beer one Saturday evening, then he found Jessica who was more voluptuous but his first tryst with Caro proved addictive. She broke her alabaster box for him, dragged her Peruvian hair at his feet and took him to the zenith of carnal pleasures, in ways he never explored with Clara. Caro stalked him in and out of the City Sports Cub chalet, with racy photo-messages and conversations on Twitter around trending issues that never closed. Caro became the deadly itch he scratched for comfort and for which he sought no cure.

Caro's idea of celebrating the New Year when 2013 arrived was to send a one-feet greeting card with "Happy New Year" emblazoned in enlarged Book Antiqua fonts and a handwritten sentence screaming on the centre-page: WE ARE PREGNANT! She signed it in the most luscious way she could: Dark Duchess.

Intersection

Mama Mechi cleaned her ears out with a match-stick as Clara walked into the kitchen. It was the third day since her arrival, the third day since she refused to allow her as much as boil her bathing water, let alone enter her room to make her bed. She wore a scowl like a fixed makeup. She reminded Clara of a void left by her mum's death ten years before, an emptiness that Mechi always promised to fill many nights of their honeymoon trip when she mentioned her mother's absence on her daughter's most important day. Clara had spent the better part of two hours since she returned from work cooking. Mechi was home early for the third straight day, always with a quick smile and a pregnant look. He still ate her meals and managed little talk, only his mother did neither. As she served Mechi's portion, Mama Mechi's look met her eyes and made to speak but changed her mind before the first word came out. Clara chose not to prod.

As the signature tune for the 9pm network news drilled into the thick cloak of silence that shielded the dining section of the living room, the doorbell rang repeatedly, smirking of impatience. Mama Mechi sprang up from her chair and headed for the door before Mechi and Clara could get in erect positions. She returned with Dr. Ogenyi, her eldest brother and Mechi's most educated uncle based in Lagos. Dr. Ogenyi exchanged greetings with Mama Mechi in their dialect, both laughing animatedly as she helped him with his little travel-box. Mechi rose up to greet him and retrieve his travel-box from his mother, Clara following him with surprise etched into her trimmed brows. She studied Mechi's face for the slightest tinge of shock at his uncle's august visit but found none. It became clear to her that there was something yet unrevealed as unclear as it was to her like the highway on a January harmattan morning.

The mass of grey hair on Uncle Ogenyi's head had

doubled since the last time they were at his house on the outskirts of Lagos to celebrate his 60th birthday so when he spoke, a natural halo seemed to crown his words, even when he jested. He asked Clara to sit with him for a few minutes then announced he was changing his mind to avoid encroaching on Mechi's territory. Everyone smiled. He began slowly, picking his words like they were hot yam slices. He called her his daughter, their wife and an invaluable addition to their family. He spoke of her husband's love for her and then his role in the Anayo family as the first son. Every word that followed came with twice the drawl he intended as they bobbled through Clara's ears. Mama Mechi had the look of a satisfied hen watching her owner club a vulture to death. Clara's eyes pierced through Mechi's wry smile, counting his canine. She returned her gaze to Uncle Ogenyi, a quarter of her listening and the rest boiling within. She knew it before he finished. Fury buoyed her feet up a few seconds, her right hand went up and returned hard on Mechi's face. It happened in a flash and he could swear he saw components of the Milky Way in that instant. Uncle Ogenyi barked him down as he made to stand up, and got in his mother's way.

"*You filthy scum-bag,*" Clara raged. "*Now, you finally got someone pregnant, happy now right?*" She had never seen herself so infuriated. Her usual calm demeanour struggled to come to the surface but couldn't. Even Uncle Ogenyi felt she had a right to vent, he only scratched his sea of grey hairs, hoping for some quick quietness so he could conclude the discussion of Clara's exalted role. Clara would have none of that. "*I hope you got some disease too,*" she spat at Mechi as she made for their bedroom. Mama Mechi got up to hold her but soon crashed into the sofa from Clara's push. Mechi got up and followed her, he had had enough of her insolence over what everyone considered a little matter.

Redemption

Six months of waiting for advice from the Director of Public Prosecution, another six months that witnessed only two appearances in court followed by three months of frequent appearances before yet another long lay-off. Mechi's trial finally came to a climax twenty-one months after it began. Beads of sweat inflated and crawled into rivulets streaming down his head and all through his body even down to his under-shorts. He glanced across the courtroom from the dock, Caro rubbed Devon's head in the back. She brought him to see him once in the Prison, when he clocked a year. He had his dimple, his small earlobe and a set of teeth that refused to close fully at the centre. Caro had that forlorn look. The lines on her face and flabby tummy made her look half a circle different from the maiden he often immersed himself with in a vortex of carnal gratification at Roots Hotel, often setting the tone from his Twitter direct message. The dark duchess was fast losing her youthful lure. Handling Devon's birth alone in Mechi's absence was taking an evident toll on her skin.

As the judge reviewed every single piece of evidence adduced before the court in the course of trial, Mechi looked towards his lawyer. Okafor gave him a confident nod and turned his face to the judge, Mechi did the same. Justice Omolola mentioned exhibit E3, the autopsy report. It stated Clara died of hemorrhage caused by cranial bleeding and trauma caused by a forceful hit to the occipital lobe. It was admitted and uncontroverted in the course of trial. She mentioned other items adduced, considered the merits of the argument and the final addresses of both prosecution and defence counsel, and then looked up. Mechi felt darts shooting at him from Justice Omolola's bespectacled face. He remembered Clara walking out on Uncle Ogenyi and his mother. He remembered himself following her into the bedroom, trying to hold his anger at her fury, he remembered it all now. He broke within, tears began to drip down his face, joining with the pond of sweat gathered on his chest. The moment her second slap stung his face like a thousand bees tore through his memory, weaving through a tunnel to the darkest end where he pushed her. He only meant to push her. He never thought she would be so light as to fall backwards till she hit her head on the wardrobe knob. Even, he was yet to understand how such a contact could make her sigh heavily, close her eyes and open them no more. He loved her; they were just going through a rough patch. He told the court the truth about everything, how much he loved her and how he strayed, even admitting that he pushed her but he had no such dark intentions. He merely wanted one more chance to redeem his love for her, one more chance to honour the memories of their love and her memory. Clara's brother would however have none of that and he was glad the State through the Prosecution team had no emotions for forgiveness.

"...I hereby sentence the accused to life imprisonment, I rise!" The judge's words cut through him like a knife. He wanted to be forgiven but he was thankful at the chance to continue to breathe, to think of Devon and of Clara and be hopeful of a pardon someday. A momentous wail tore through the courtroom and in the midst of the roar, the names of his mother, Uncle Ogenyi and every other member of his family dropped in his pacing heart. He looked towards their corner. Mama Mechi was in tears, being consoled by her friends who came in solidarity. Uncle Ogenyi looked into space, Devon seated on his laps and an empty space where Caro sat earlier, to his left. Mechi sighed. His tears ceased. He stretched forth his hands to the Corporal and Prison Official dangling a manacle before him. He looked into their faces and whispered "Redeem me!"

Retrospection

Sometime ago, as I sat with a friend in a bid to gormandize a late lunch , he pointed to a house on the other side of the road that houses his friend, the same house had once housed his friend's father.

We chatted for a while and he pointed me to what I had missed by his showing of the bequeathed house of his friend to me. He told me a lot of us attach outlandish importance to material things like our lives depend on them. Materials that we'll in the end leave as we shall pass. There is no crime in living a cozy life but a human form should always aspire for a better fulfillment than materialism.

Let ephemeral be to the ephemeral and let lasting legacies be entrenched on the minds and on the hearts of the people around us.

Our neighbours are usually people that are affected in one way or the other by our actions or inactions.